PIVOT POINT

PIVOT POINT FUNDAMENTALS: ESTHETICS
FACIAL TREATMENTS

©2020 Pivot Point International, Inc.
All Rights Reserved.
ISBN 978-1-951862-21-3

1st Edition
1st Printing, December 2020
Printed in USA

This publication is protected under U.S. and worldwide copyright laws and may not be copied, reproduced, stored in a retrieval system, transmitted, broadcast or quoted in whole or in part in any form, or by any means: electronically or mechanically, printed, photocopied, recorded, scanned or otherwise, nor may derivative works be created from it, without written permission from Pivot Point International, Inc. More detailed information on copyright can be found at http://www.pivot-point.com/copyright.html

Pivot Point is a registered trademark and *Pivot Point Fundamentals* is a trademark of Pivot Point International, Inc. in the United States and other countries, and may not be used or reproduced in any manner without expressed written consent.

Pivot Point International, Inc.
Global Headquarters
8725 West Higgins Road, Suite 700
Chicago, IL 60631 USA

847-866-0500
pivot-point.com

CONTENTS
107ᴱ // FACIAL TREATMENTS

Facial Treatment Theory	2
Facial Treatment Products, Tools, Supplies and Equipment	16
Facial Treatment Skills	34
Facial Treatment Guest Experience	59
Draping, Towel and Table Preparation for Facial Treatment Skills Workshop	89
Pre-cleanse Skills Workshop	96
Skin Analysis Skills Workshop	100
Cleanse and Tone Skills Workshop	105

Mechanical Exfoliation and Extraction Skills Workshop	109
Massage Skills Workshop	114
Mask and Protect Skills Workshop	122
Basic Facial Treatment Workshop	127
Men's Facial Treatment Workshop	138
Acne Facial Treatment Workshop	148
Chemical Exfoliation	158
Chemical Exfoliation Workshop	195

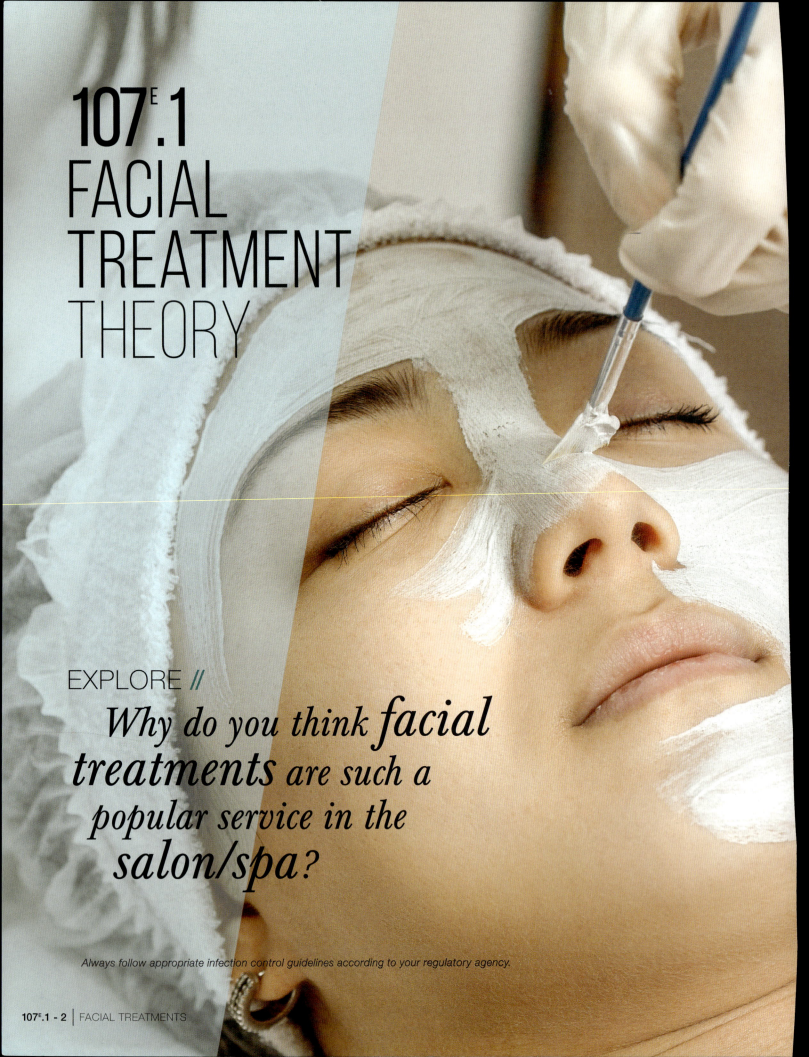

107E.1 FACIAL TREATMENT THEORY

EXPLORE //

Why do you think facial treatments are such a popular service in the salon/spa?

Always follow appropriate infection control guidelines according to your regulatory agency.

INSPIRE //

Facial treatments are considered the "bread and butter" service of the spa. Your ability to understand client concerns and create a relaxing experience is key to achieving repeat clients.

ACHIEVE //

Following this lesson on *Facial Treatment Theory*, you'll be able to:

» List the various types of facial treatment services offered in the salon/spa

» Identify the benefits of facial treatment services

FOCUS //

FACIAL TREATMENT THEORY

Facial Treatment Services

Facial Treatment Benefits

Skin appearance is a mirror of physical and emotional well-being. People communicate with you and learn to know you by reading your face. Skin tends to glow when a person is happy and healthy or may look sallow and dull when sad or in poor health. The facial service is a tremendous stress-reliever and a way for clients to take time out for themselves. It's relaxing, rejuvenating and refreshing, as well as a path to better skin health. Once you see the effect your facial service has on clients, you'll naturally be motivated to perfect your skills to deliver this very popular service!

Always follow appropriate infection control guidelines according to your regulatory agency.

FACIAL TREATMENT SERVICES

A facial treatment is a service used to improve and maintain the appearance of the face skin. Also called "facial," they use various, often customized techniques, such as deep cleansing, exfoliation, hydration and stimulation of the skin.

Facial treatments are called "bread and butter" treatments because they strengthen the entire service menu. Facials are often the most requested services and can produce the highest profit margin.

Facial methods can differ, and most skin care companies have a specific protocol for application to include specialized techniques for a unique result.

Equipment can be used; however, the skill of the esthetician's hands is the most effective tool, as they can personalize their techniques for each client.

Each facial's variations will depend on the client's needs, skin type and any conditions, as well as time limitations. Common types of facials you will perform in the salon/spa include:

» Facial treatment
» Express facial treatment
» Acne facial treatment
» Men's facial treatment
» Anti-aging facial treatment
» Hydrating facial treatment

FACIAL TREATMENT

The facial treatment will play a key role in your daily schedule, and can be commonly called the "European facial," "basic facial," "classic facial" or any specialty name the salon/spa uses. The duration of the facial is what counts when considering different types of facials. The facial treatment that you will learn is based on a 60-minute service, and it's best to sharpen and perfect your facial steps early on in your career.

A facial treatment includes these fundamental steps or a variation based on the manufacturer products being used:

» Pre-Cleanse   » Treat
» Analyze   » Massage
» Cleanse and Tone   » Mask
» Exfoliate   » Protect

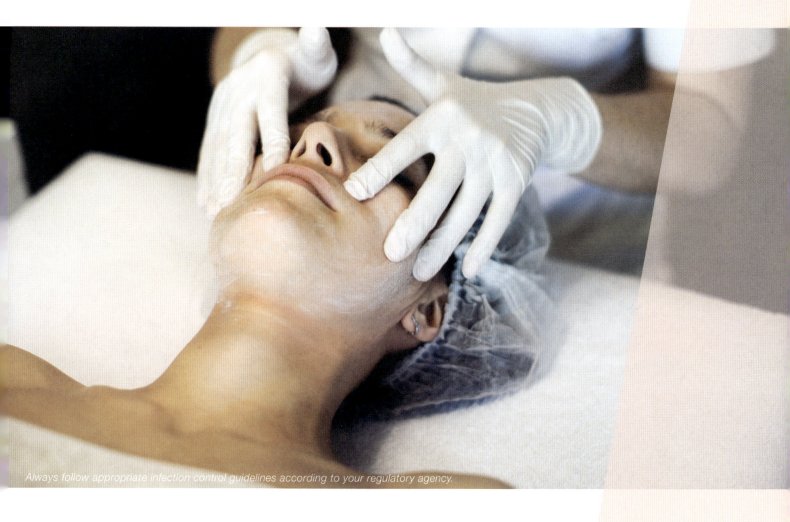

Always follow appropriate infection control guidelines according to your regulatory agency.

FACIAL TREATMENT PHASES

You may recall in the lesson on the *Skin Assessment and Recommendation System* that the information you gather from the client's skin assessment is used to customize the protocol you deliver to meet their unique needs. You may also recall that the facial treatment is divided into three phases, with each having a specific purpose. These three phases are identified by the impact each has on the skin and includes:

- Increase phase
- Balance phase
- Decrease phase

Each phase is delivered using the basic steps to carry out a customized protocol for each client; the order of these steps can be changed for some protocols. An example is a 60-minute facial that includes extraction in the Treat step, often the massage step is moved before the extraction to avoid spreading bacteria and causing further breakouts. Another example is adding a non-setting clay mask into the steps to further draw impurities to the skin's surface.

INCREASE PHASE

As mentioned in the *Skin Assessment and Recommendation System* lesson, think of the Increase phase like the "warm-up" of a workout. The function of the Increase phase is to stimulate the skin, promoting cell turnover and increased skin moisture. The following are the facial treatment steps and their functions involved in the Increase phase:

Pre-Cleanse	Light cleansing to remove any makeup
Analyze	Assessment of the skin to create a personalized treatment
Cleanse and Tone	Deep cleansing; refreshes the skin and balances the pH; skin warming to soften skin
Exfoliate	Removal of dead skin cells and build-up of pollution and debris; steam to activate an enzyme exfoliation

⚡ BALANCE PHASE

After you stimulate the skin, it is ready to begin the Balance phase. During this phase, the skin is prepared to receive an infusion of active ingredients to correct the skin's pH and improve the skin's hydration and protection. The modalities used to balance the skin vary depending on each client's skin analysis. You'll use the following steps and their functions during the Balance phase:

Treat	Extractions to remove comedones; antibacterial product; specific condition serum
Massage	Provides nutrients to the skin, initiates relaxation, increases microcirculation and serum absorption

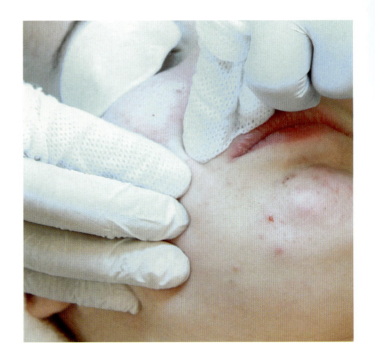

⚡ DECREASE PHASE

After the skin is balanced to improve its pH, hydration and protection, the skin should be calmed and sedated. The goals of the Decrease phase are to:

» Reduce inflammation, microcirculation, and bacteria overgrowth

» Target pigmentation concerns, erythema (redness), rough texture and edema

» Decrease skin barrier dysfunction and melanocyte over-production

Refer to the *Skin Assessment and Recommendation* System lesson for more on how each phase of the facial treatment relates to various categories of skin conditions.

You'll use the following steps and their functions during the Decrease phase:

Mask	Specialized ingredients to enhance, calm the skin and focus on the skin's concerns
Protect	Add serums to address specific concerns and moisturize with sun protection (SPF)

EXPRESS FACIAL TREATMENT

Many salon/spas offer a condensed, 30-minute facial, often called an "express facial" or "mini-facial." This treatment has grown in popularity, especially for busy people during a lunch hour.

The express facial is a speedy version of a facial treatment. It should not replace the monthly facial treatment that works much deeper and is more specialized to the client's skin care concerns.

With the express facial, the Balance phase is usually omitted, but in some cases, the massage replaces the mask. If you are building your business and would like to demonstrate your massage skill, it is acceptable to change this if you have the approval to do so.

Generally, these facials are given with the client's immediate concerns in mind, for instance, dullness or a sudden breakout of papules or pustules. The express facial refreshes the skin and gives it a boost.

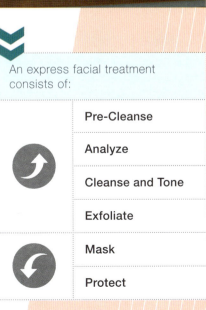

An express facial treatment consists of:

- Pre-Cleanse
- Analyze
- Cleanse and Tone
- Exfoliate
- Mask
- Protect

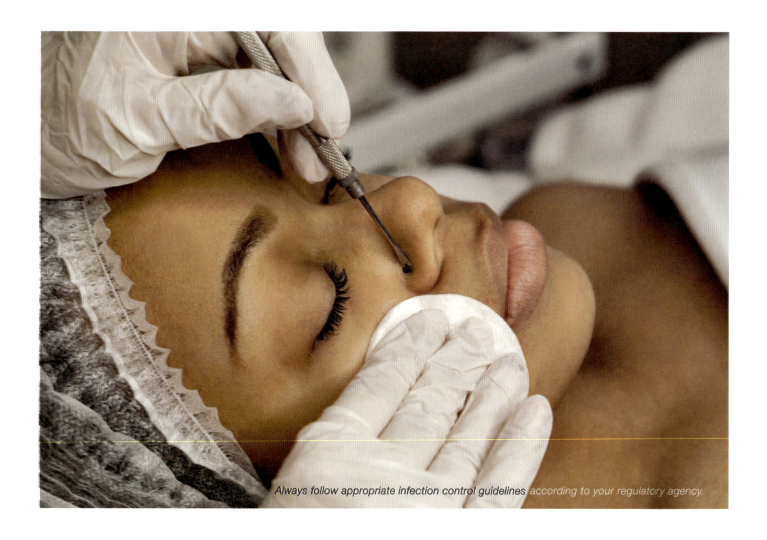

Always follow appropriate infection control guidelines according to your regulatory agency.

ACNE FACIAL TREATMENT

Acne facial treatments are very popular in salon/spas and medical environments. The steps of the facial vary based on the products you use and the grade of acne. During the Balance phase, the massage should avoid inflamed, acneic areas.

As you learned in the *Skin* area of study, there are different grades of acne. It is common for clients with Grades 1/2 acne to receive acne facials without a physician's consent. However, clients with Grades 3/4 require physician consent prior to service, due to inflammation and severe infection, causing long-term scarring. There is also a possibility the client will have eruptions on their chest and/or back.

There are some points to consider prior to performing an acne facial that could affect the service, including:

Consideration		Affect
Is the client under a doctor's care for acne?	»	Topical acne medication is a contraindication for many products such as benzoyl peroxide
Has your client been diagnosed with reproductive health issues such as polycystic ovary syndrome (PCOS)?	»	If present, this disorder must be treated to see any reduction in acne

In general, an acne facial treatment will include:

- Pre-Cleanse
- Analyze
- Cleanse and Tone
- Exfoliate
- **Extraction**
- Mask
- Protect

The following guidelines should be followed during certain steps of an acne facial treatment.

Exfoliate	»	Never use physical or mechanical exfoliation on inflamed acne
	»	Use enzyme masks for exfoliation
Extraction	»	Do not try to extract papules
	»	Lancets on pustules can only be used if your area's regulatory agency allows it; use sterilized lancets only
	»	Do not do extensive extractions on dehydrated skin; keep it under 5 minutes to avoid damage
	»	Always use an anti-bacterial product after extraction
Massage	»	Do not perform facial massage on inflamed acne
Mask	»	Ingredients helpful for acne are:
		» High-antioxidant botanicals such as green tea, blueberry, pomegranate
		» Salicylic acid
		» Chocolate
		» Sulfur
		» Zinc
		» Bentonite clay
		» Sea salt
	»	Do not apply warm towel to remove mask

Acne treatments will benefit from the use of devices such as high frequency, galvanic and LED light therapy. You will learn about facial treatment devices in the *Facial Treatments With Devices* area of study.

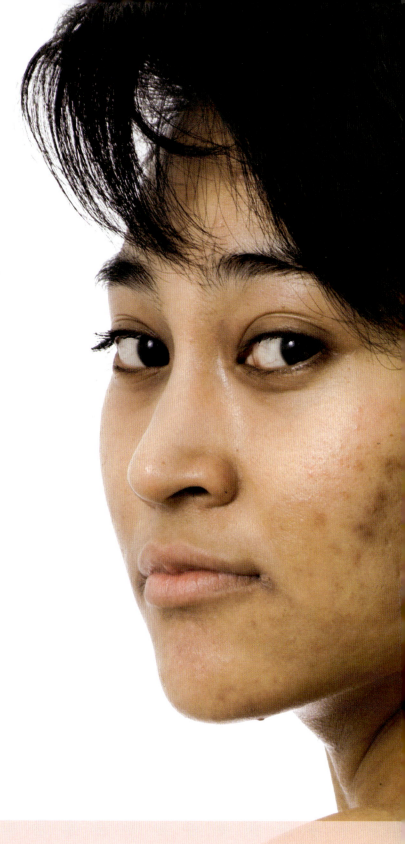

Using Esthetics Devices
All the facial protocols you will learn can be adapted to include facial devices such as steamers, rotating brush, galvanic current and other devices. What you can use depends on the scope of practice your regulatory agency allows. When using any devices, thoroughly understanding them is essential. The results you can expect from using devices are enhanced if you use them correctly. You will learn more about devices in the *Facial Treatments With Devices* area of study.

MEN'S FACIAL TREATMENT

Many men are interested in properly caring for their skin. The goal is the same for men as it is for women, and the facial treatment is essentially the same; the only difference is in techniques. If you master the facial treatment, you will be able to do a men's facial when you address what your male client needs.

There are some differences in men's skin that you need to take into consideration when performing a men's facial. They are:

- The skin – pH of a male client tends to be more acidic
- Facial hair – Often thick and issues with folliculitis
- Oil production – Testosterone promotes an active sebaceous gland

Some common bacterial and fungal infections to be aware of that relate to men's facial hair include:

Folliculitis Barbae (fah-lik-yuh-LY-tis BAR-bay)

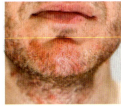

- Commonly referred to as "barber's itch"; an infection on the face and neck where the area surrounding the hair follicle is inflamed with redness and pustules
- Caused by damage or blockage of the hair follicle, usually due to incorrect shaving
- Refer client to a physician; usually treated with a topical or oral anti-staphylococcal antibiotic

Pseudofolliculitis Barbae (SOO-doe-fah-lik-yuh-LY-tis BAR-bay)

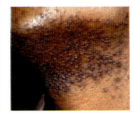

- Also known as shaving rash or razor bumps; foreign body reaction
- Characterized by papules, which may be itchy
- Occurs most often in men with coarse or tightly curled hair in which the hair curves back into the skin, creating inflammation of the hair follicles
- Caused by ingrown hair due to incorrect shaving
- Many products on the market specifically for pseudofolliculitis barbae
- Exfoliate using gentle scrub to remove dead skin cells and soften skin

Always follow appropriate infection control guidelines according to your regulatory agency.

With that in mind, here are some additional guidelines to follow during a men's facial treatment:

Exfoliate	»	Skin benefits from an exfoliant or enzyme treatment with an acidic pH
	»	Bearded man – Use gel in the beard area because thick cream or clay masks are difficult to remove
	»	Use circular movements to reach the base of follicle.
Treat	»	Use steam and desincrustation product to soften debris before extraction
	»	Use fingers or comedone remover tool
	»	Avoid trying to remove every comedone with the first treatment; it could cause damage to the skin
Eye Products	»	Use a firming product with anti-aging ingredients
Massage	»	Movement should be performed in a downward circular movement through the beard area
	»	Be sure to check in on their comfort level
	»	Beard oil is very beneficial during the massage
Mask	»	Use a soothing and/or hydrating mask since men are unlikely to use moisturizers
	»	Beard area – Use a gel mask for easy removal

Note: The use of warm steaming towels to remove exfoliants and masks is also helpful.

Deciding whether to use equipment during men's facials may depend on the amount of facial hair. Still, the rotating brush and toner spray can usually be utilized with successful results.

INDUSTRY CONNECTION

Home Care for Men
Men can benefit from the same products women use. They tend to like one-step cleansing and toning (which can also replace the use of aftershave) and simple home-care procedures.

However, you may be surprised at the number of men willing to commit to entire treatment lines such as eye products, exfoliants, masks and creams. Your professional knowledge and skill will influence their decision to care for their skin at home.

Keep in mind that male clients are more concerned with simple basic products as opposed to fragrances, colors and pretty packages. Clearly marked, easy-to-use tubes are great sellers!

» As more men become aware of the need to care for their skin, they are becoming loyal, dedicated clients. Today, a growing percentage of men look to estheticians to meet their skin care needs.

FACIAL TREATMENT BENEFITS

Facials are an essential skill for you to master as an esthetician, since performing them well will keep clients coming back. Be sure to customize them for each client's skin care needs, so they can see and feel the benefits. Your client can experience a variety of benefits from professional facial services, including:

- Relaxed muscles
- Soothed nerves
- Hydrated skin
- Improved circulation
- Enhanced health of the skin
- Overall relaxation
- Blemish improvement
- Reduced redness
- Skin brightening

Always follow appropriate infection control guidelines according to your regulatory agency.

TYPES OF FACIAL TREATMENTS

Although facials have general overall benefits, various types of facials focus on the existing skin conditions of each client. You, as the esthetician, will have the knowledge to make the most comprehensive decision about which type of facial will be more beneficial.

TYPES OF FACIALS	EXISTING CONDITION OF SKIN	BENEFITS
Anti-Aging Facials	» Dull appearance » Enlarged pores » Sagging skin » Wrinkles » Discoloration and redness » Congested skin	» Firming and toning » Deep exfoliation » Increased hydration » Improved skin clarity
Acne Facials	» Grade 1 acne » Grade 2 acne » Papules » Pustules » Inflammation » Blackheads » Comedones » Milia » Oiliness	» Deep cleansing » Exfoliation » Bacteria overgrowth control » Extraction » Oil control
Soothing Facials	» Redness » Dryness/flakiness » Dehydration » Irritated skin » Edema	» Reduction of redness » Reduction of irritation » Deep hydration
Skin-Brightening Facials	» Hyperpigmentation (dark spots) » UV damage » Dull skin » Patches of discoloration » Dull appearance	» Reduction of dark spots » Increased hydration » Deep exfoliation
Hydrating Facials	» Dry » Dehydrated » Fine lines » Redness	» Increased hydration » Relaxation » Light exfoliation
Post-Surgery Facials (used in medical settings)	» Erythema » Edema » Bruising » Under doctor's care	» Reduced discomfort » Increase lymphatic drainage » Deep hydration

No matter the type of facial, there will be specific steps or phases of the facial that directly impact how the skin reacts. Once you master the skills to do a correct skin analysis, you'll more easily choose the correct facial to perform. Your choice will be based on your client's concerns and the current state of their skin. The main purpose of any facial treatment is to improve the client's overall skin health. Facials are an effective way to improve skin health when performed consistently.

EFFECT ON SKIN HEALTH

As an esthetician, you need to be able to recognize the visual signs of unhealthy skin as it relates to the skin's color, texture and hydration. Any sensation that a client regularly experiences is also a sign of skin health. Being able to explain the effects a professional program has on your clients' skin is important. The following chart identifies the signs of unhealthy skin, in several categories and the recommended facial treatment.

CATEGORIES	UNHEALTHY SKIN	RECOMMENDED FACIAL TREATMENTS	RESULT AFTER SEVERAL TREATMENTS
Color	Uneven color, hyperpigmentation or UV damage	» Skin-brightening facial » Anti-aging facial	» Even color; minimal or no hyperpigmentation or UV damage
Texture	Blemishes, or rough-textured, congested skin	» Acne facial » Soothing facial	» Reduced or no blemishes » Smoother texture
Hydration	Flaking, fine lines, dry, dehydrated, dull TEWL*	» Hydrating facial	» Minimal to no flaking or fine lines » Radiant, glowing skin
Sensation	Itching, burning or general irritation	» Hydrating facial » Soothing facial	» No itching, burning or general irritation

*Transepidermal water loss

Facial treatments are primarily determined by the manufacturer protocol you follow and the products you use. There are common steps that each protocol uses. As you gain experience you will be able to customize any treatment based on the skin analysis, benefits to the client's skin health and the client's desired benefits.

What's on the Menu?

From the "Caviar Facial" to the "Vampire Facial," spas and salons around the world create customized facial treatments to not only cater to clients' specific needs but also create a unique experience. While some may seem a little bizarre, as with the "Snail Facial," some salon/spas create facial treatments that are unique to their brand. Explore the many types of facial treatments being offered in your area—nationally and even internationally.

Always follow appropriate infection control guidelines according to your regulatory agency.

FREQUENCY OF TREATMENT

Regular facial treatments promote the overall health of the skin. After a facial, the skin generally looks and feels good for about a week. Understanding how often to recommend facial treatments is an important part of creating a treatment plan. Frequency is often tied to requested results. For example, if you are performing treatments for hyperpigmentation, this needs to be done at least every two weeks for the first 120 days (4 months). Depending on the client's age, this could be up to 8 treatments.

The length of time depends on the skin assessment and goals the client wants to achieve. A typical course of services is in blocks of three months. If improvement is not seen within that period, the skin assessment, home skin care and protocol choices should be reviewed.

When facials are more regular, the longevity of the effects improves and can give a continuous healthy appearance. This enables the esthetician to work less on repair and more with maintenance, protection and prevention.

Here is a quick summary of the frequency to plan facials. For more information, refer to the *Skin Analysis and Recommendation System* lesson.

> Healthy skin maintenance/stress reduction: *Every 4 weeks*

> Problem correction; *Every 2 weeks*

> **Note:** All chemical exfoliation treatments, such as a glycolic peel, should never be closer together than two weeks due to the desquamation process in the skin.

Understanding the various types of facial treatments and the benefits they offer will give you the fundamentals needed for the most requested services in the salon/spa.

LESSONS LEARNED

Facial treatment services offered in the salon/spa include:

- Facial treatment
- Express facial treatment
- Acne facial treatment
- Men's facial treatment

Benefits of facial treatments include:

- Relaxed muscles
- Soothed nerves
- Hydrated skin
- Improved circulation
- Enhanced health of the skin
- Overall relaxation
- Blemish improvement
- Reduced redness
- Skin brightening

107E.2 FACIAL TREATMENT
PRODUCTS, TOOLS, SUPPLIES AND EQUIPMENT

EXPLORE //
What do you think your favorite product will be to use during facial treatments?

INSPIRE //

Facial treatment products, tools, supplies and equipment support the most requested service in the salon/spa.

ACHIEVE //

Following this lesson on *Facial Treatment Products, Tools, Supplies and Equipment*, you'll be able to:

» Identify the function of facial treatment products

» Describe the function and infection control guidelines for tools and supplies used for facial treatments

» Explain the function and infection control guidelines for equipment used for facial treatments

FOCUS //

FACIAL TREATMENT PRODUCTS, TOOLS, SUPPLIES AND EQUIPMENT

Facial Treatment Products

Facial Treatment Tools and Supplies

Facial Treatment Equipment

The right tools, supplies and equipment for the treatment is crucial to the smooth running of the salon/spa. You'll need to have a good understanding of the roles, benefits and effects of each. Your treatment results are influenced by the products, tools and equipment you use, so knowing the correct use for each item helps you determine how to customize your services.

FACIAL TREATMENT PRODUCTS

The products used for a professional treatment are usually the same products that are used in a home-care routine. The only difference is professional-only products are designed specifically for use in the treatment room. Details about each type of product (except professional-only products) are in the lesson on *Cosmetic Products*.

FACIAL TREATMENT MAKEUP REMOVERS

The first step in the facial procedure is to remove makeup and debris. This is also known as the first cleanse, or pre-cleanse, and is done regardless of makeup being present. Makeup removers can be substituted by gentle non-foaming cleansers. The goal is to clean the skin enough to do a skin assessment.

PRODUCTS	PROFESSIONAL USE	WHEN TO USE
Oily	» Use for waterproof or water-resistant makeup. » Dispense into a cotton round and place on eyes.	Pre-Cleanse
Non-Oily	» Use for all makeup removal except waterproof. » Use on entire face to remove foundation and perform the first cleanse. » Dispense into a bowl and apply with a brush or fingers.	

FACIAL TREATMENT CLEANSERS

Facial cleansers are used in the second cleanse, or Cleanse and Tone step of the facial. Often the cleansers used in a treatment are different from the cleansers that will be used in the client's home-care routine. The goal is usually to deep-cleanse, using stronger cleanser than recommended for daily use. An example is a cleansing gel on all skin types before a chemical exfoliation.

PRODUCTS	PROFESSIONAL USE	WHEN TO USE
Cleansing Milk	» Use for second cleanse; all skin types. » Dispense into small bowl, apply with brush or hands. » Perform cleansing massage movements. » Remove with disposable sponge, gauze or warm towel.	Cleanse and Tone
Cleansing Cream	» Use for second cleanse; dry, normal skin types. » Dispense into small bowl, apply with brush or hands. » Perform cleansing massage movements. » Remove with disposable sponges, non-woven gauze or warm towels.	
Facial Wash/ Cleansing Gel	» Use for second cleanse; all skin types; prep for chemical or mechanical exfoliation. » Dispense small amount in bowl, use brush to whip; apply to face. » Perform cleansing massage or use rotating brush. » Remove with warm towels or disposable sponges.	

Cosmetic Ingredients

Estheticians should be familiar with the most commonly used cosmetic ingredients and their functions. Skin care companies offer training to ensure you choose correct products to correct skin concerns. Each ingredient has a special name that is recognized internationally as INCI (which stands for the International Nomenclature of Cosmetic Ingredients). INCI helps eliminate any confusion on universally known ingredients, so you can recommend products with a clear understanding. Refer to the lesson *Cosmetic Product Ingredients* for detailed information.

FACIAL TREATMENT TONERS

Toners are primarily for pH balancing and hydration, after the second cleanse and after mask removal. Toners come in spray forms, and you can apply them directly on the skin or on saturated cotton pads. They need to be appropriate for the skin type and condition. For a professional facial treatment, you can use toners that provide a specific benefit, with some that deliver active ingredients like peptides into the skin.

PRODUCTS	PROFESSIONAL USE	WHEN TO USE
Toning Lotion	» Use after second cleanse and after mask; combination, normal skin. » Dispense into a cotton round or spray over face. » Blot excess toner with a tissue. » Do not remove.	Cleanse and Tone
Tonic	» Use after second cleanse, after mask; all skin types; no sensitive skin conditions. » Dispense into a cotton round or spray on face. » Blot excess with a tissue. » Do not remove.	Cleanse and Tone Mask
Astringent	» Use after second cleanse, after extraction; combination, oily, acne-prone skin. » Dispense into a cotton round. » Do not remove or blot.	Cleanse and Tone Treat

FACIAL TREATMENT EXFOLIANTS

Exfoliation is extremely important in a facial, as it helps the absorption of products and improves cellular renewal. All skin types can be exfoliated. The differences will be the frequency and the type of exfoliant used, the Fitzpatrick skin type and any sensitive skin conditions.

PRODUCTS	PROFESSIONAL USE	WHEN TO USE
Enzyme	» Dispense enough to cover upper chest, neck and face, mix according to manufacturer's instructions. » Perform enzyme exfoliation using steam for a minimum of 10 minutes; hot towels may be used to replace steam. » Remove with disposable sponges, gauze or warm towels.	Exfoliate *All Fitzpatrick types allowed* *Considered a chemical exfoliant*
Scrub	» Don't use on sensitive skin conditions. » Dispense according to manufacturer's instructions; apply a thin layer. » Perform cleansing movements from upper chest, neck and face; use lighter touch on neck and chest. » Remove with warm towels.	Exfoliate *Use caution with Fitzpatrick types 5-6* *Considered a mechanical exfoliant*
Exfoliating Cream *(Also known as gommage)*	» Don't use on sensitive skin conditions. » Dispense into a small bowl. » Apply in a thin layer with a mask brush, let dry; no steam. » Perform gentle circular rubbing movements from neck to forehead. » Remove with a warm towel.	Exfoliate *All Fitzpatrick types allowed* *Considered a mechanical exfoliant*
Acid Exfoliant	» Type of acid is based on skin conditions and Fitzpatrick type. » Dispense per manufacturer's instructions. » Additional training is mandatory.	Stand-alone treatment *Use caution with Fitzpatrick types 4-6* *Considered a chemical exfoliant*
Desincrustation Solution	» Use before extraction to soften debris. » Apply thin layer over areas to extract. » Apply steam for at least 3 minutes » Use with galvanic current desincrustation (see the lesson on *Facial Treatment With Devices Skills*)	Treat *Use for extraction*

FACIAL TREATMENT MASSAGE MEDIUMS

Massage mediums such as creams, oils or gels provide "slip" (reduce friction) during massage. Some mediums help deliver nutrients to the skin as well. Be sure to use the correct amount to help avoid too much absorption, which will interrupt the flow of your massage.

PRODUCTS	PROFESSIONAL USE	WHEN TO USE
Oil	» Use on all skin types except oily; all conditions except acne. » Dispense a generous amount and apply with brush or hands to chest, neck and face. » Choose massage movements based on skin concern; works well with longer massage routines. » Remove excess with gauze or tissue. Note: Do not apply serums after oil-based massage mediums.	Massage step *Aromatherapy oils can be added*
Cream	» Use on all skin types except oily; all conditions except acne. Good for clients who dislike oil. » Dispense moderate amount; apply with hands. » Use massage movements; may absorb quicker into skin; limit length of massage or re-apply medium. » Remove excess with cool towel or disposable sponge.	Massage step *Hand and arm massage*
Gel	» Use on oily or combination skin, acne and rosacea conditions. » Dispense generous amount; apply with hands. » Use pressure-point massage, light effleurage. » Do not remove; leaves no residue.	Massage step

FACIAL TREATMENT MASKS

A mask can be designed to hydrate, soothe, tighten pores, gently exfoliate, reduce excess oil, improve absorption of active ingredients or offer nourishment to the skin. Masks should not be applied in a thin layer, so use the correct amount—you should not see the skin underneath. Masks should provide an occlusive layer to help active ingredients absorb into the skin. Always apply a mask to the upper chest and neck as well.

PRODUCTS	PROFESSIONAL USE	WHEN TO USE
Setting Masks	**Clay/Mud** » Use to absorb excess oil, dislodge debris, mildly exfoliate; not for dry, dehydrated skin. » Dispense a generous amount; apply thickly in areas to deep-clean. » Remove with warm towels.	Mask step
	Peel-Off (Modeling) » Use for serum absorption, firming and hydration; all skin types. » Dispense according to manufacturer's instructions; mix quickly and apply in thick layer over face and neck; avoid eye area. » Pull off, then remove residue with gauze.	After Treat step
	Thermal Mask » Use to absorb serums and tighten skin; do not use on sensitive skin conditions. » Dispense according to manufacturer's instructions, mix quickly and apply in thick layer. » Remove after mask hardens and cools, after 20 minutes; there should be no residue.	
	Paraffin (Warm Wax) » Use to hydrate, increase product absorption; do not use on sensitive skin conditions. » Dispense a generous amount and apply to face, neck and chest with brush or dip gauze mask in paraffin dip then apply on face. » Remove after paraffin hardens and cools.	
	Sheet Mask » Use to hydrate, firm and lift; all skin types. Do not use on acne skin conditions unless specifically designed to treat. » Dispense following manufacturer's instructions; apply with fingers. » Remove after mask sets, usually 10-15 minutes; do not remove residue, if any.	
Non-Setting Masks	**Cream Mask** » Use to hydrate, calm and soothe skin; dry skin and aging, sensitive skin conditions. » Dispense generously and apply thickly with a face fan brush. » Remove with warm towels or disposable sponges.	Mask step
	Gel » Use to hydrate, reduce fine lines and calm; all skin types. » Dispense a generous amount and apply in a thick layer with a mask brush. » Remove with warm or cool towel, or disposable sponges. » Use as a coupling gel for electrical devices.	After Treat step

Multi-Masking

Multi-masking uses different masks in specific areas on the face for a customized treatment. For example, you may use a clay setting mask in the T-zone with a hydrating cream mask on the neck, chest and rest of the face. It is an effective way to address multiple issues and provide a client-focused treatment.

FACIAL TREATMENT SERUM

Serums used in the Treat step usually have a higher level of active ingredients. Many professional-only serums come in ampoule packaging, meaning individually sealed bottles. Other serums come in the same type of packaging as retail products but are sold only to licensed professionals. Massage, devices and masks help serums penetrate skin. Serums can treat certain conditions. Use antibacterial products to treat breakouts and reduce bacteria after an extraction in this step.

PRODUCTS	PROFESSIONAL USE	WHEN TO USE
Serum	» Use for specific skin conditions. » Dispense per manufacturer's instructions; use hands or face brush. » Perform massage movements or use galvanic current (water-based serums). » Do not remove.	Treat step
Antibacterial Serum	» Use after extraction, before mask step for breakouts » Dispense a small amount and spot treat » Do not remove.	Treat step Protect step

FACIAL TREATMENT MOISTURIZERS

Moisturizers are an important part of the Protect step. Use the day or night moisturizer that the client will use at home. This is their opportunity to see how your recommended products will work on their skin. The only difference with the moisturizer you will use at the end of the facial and professional-use manufacturer products is the size.

PRODUCTS	PROFESSIONAL USE	WHEN TO USE
Day Cream	» Dispense a small amount and apply after the serum, if applicable. » Use application movements to penetrate. » Use a night cream if an evening appointment or client needs additional hydration.	Protect step
Night Cream	» Use only if day cream is not used. » Dispense a small amount and apply after serum, if applicable. » Use application movements to penetrate.	
Lip Cream	» Use for dry lips. » Dispense a small amount; apply with fingers, disposable lip brush or cotton swab. » Use gentle application movements.	
Neck Cream	» Use for aging skin conditions. » Dispense a generous amount and apply with hands. » Use application movements upward toward jawline.	
Eye Cream or Gel	» Use for all eye conditions, all skin types. » Dispense a small amount; apply with fingertips. » Use eye movements to penetrate product.	

FACIAL TREATMENT SUNSCREENS

Apply sunscreen when a facial is done during the day. If it's a nighttime appointment, omit this step. Ideally, use a non-chemical sunscreen after a facial treatment; often the client's skin is overstimulated and can be more sensitive than normal.

PRODUCTS	PROFESSIONAL USE	WHEN TO USE
Sunscreen	» Use after moisturizers, eye cream and neck cream. » Dispense a generous amount; apply with hands. » Perform gentle application movements. » A physical sunscreen with no chemicals is best.	End of facial, during the day

DISCOVER MORE

Product and Service Claims

Clients can be uneducated about products and services. Be sure you clearly and honestly represent what your products and services do. The saying "under-promise and over-deliver" is a good rule to follow. This helps when it comes to protecting your professional reputation as well. Many states have clauses that specifically outline false advertising guidelines and misrepresentation. Here are some common pitfalls to avoid:

» Your title: Be sure to represent what your license states; a title like Medical Esthetician is not a legal designation.

» Product claims: An example is claiming that a product is organic without a legal designation such as the USDA seal, or claiming unproven results.

» Services: Avoid saying that "instant results" are possible or other results are impossible. No matter what your employer or manufacturer states, it's your integrity and your clients' trust that suffers if you misrepresent what you can do.

107E.2 | FACIAL TREATMENT PRODUCTS, TOOLS, SUPPLIES AND EQUIPMENT

FACIAL TREATMENT TOOLS AND SUPPLIES

The tools and supplies that you use for professional treatments vary based on the type of service and your personal preferences. The amount of supplies should be kept to a minimum to lower your costs and to be environmentally conscious. Remember that you need to disinfect multi-use items after every client, so it's a good idea to have multiple sets of tools when your schedule becomes full.

Cleaning means removing surface or visible debris and potential pathogens to slow the growth of pathogens. Use soap, detergent or chemical "cleaner," followed by a clean-water rinse. Cleaning is performed before disinfection procedures.

Disinfection kills certain pathogens (bacteria, viruses and fungi)—but not spores—on nonporous surfaces, tools and multi-use supplies. Disinfectants come in varied forms, including concentrate, liquid, spray or wipes that have EPA approval for use in the salon/spa industry. Immersion and disinfecting spray or wipes are common for disinfecting tools, multi-use supplies and equipment in the salon/spa. Be sure to follow the manufacturer's instructions for mixing disinfecting solutions and contact time if applicable.

Only nonporous tools, supplies and equipment can be disinfected. All single-use items must be discarded after each use. Always follow your area's regulatory guidelines, including the use of appropriate personal protective equipment (PPE).

FACIAL TREATMENT - TOOLS

TOOLS	FUNCTION	CLEANING GUIDELINES	DISINFECTION GUIDELINES
Fan Brush	» Applies product to face, neck and upper chest	» Preclean with soap and water. » Dry. » Rinse well.	» Immerse in an approved EPA-registered disinfectant solution. » Rinse well. » Allow to dry. » Store appropriately, as required by regulatory agency.
Comedone Extractor	» Used to ease the removal of comedones		
Spatula	» Removes product from containers » Helps prevent cross-contamination	» If single-use item, discard. » If multi-use item, preclean with soap and water. » Rinse well.	» If multi-use item disinfect by immersing in an approved EPA-registered disinfectant solution. » Rinse well. » Dry. » Store in clean, dry, covered container.
Bowl Large-Medium-Small	» Holds mixtures for any type of peel or mask before applying to the skin » Holds warm water for sponges or gauze, used for product removal	» Preclean with soap and water. » Rinse well.	» Immerse in an approved EPA-registered disinfectant solution. » Rinse well. » Dry. » Store in cabinet.

FACIAL TREATMENT - SUPPLIES

SUPPLIES	FUNCTION	CLEANING GUIDELINES	DISINFECTION GUIDELINES
4 X 4 Non-Woven Gauze Wipe	» Used to remove products » Does not leave lint like a cotton round » Use to remove debris from extractions » Disposable	» Single-use item, must be discarded.	» Cannot be disinfected, discard after one use.
Gauze Mask	» Used as facial mask (paraffin or other) » Used as slip for high-frequency device		
Cotton Round	» Applies/removes product » Used damp to remove products from face and neck » 4" (10.16 cm) diameter for cleansing pads » 2" (5.08 cm) diameter for individual eye pads » 2" (5.08 cm) by 6" (15.24 cm) ovals for eye pads		
Tissues	» Used to blot face after toning » Protect client's hair with setting mask; line headband » Saturated with astringent to use after extraction, if desired		
Cotton Swab	» Applies/removes product » Great for lip product application		
Single-Use Towel	» Used on supply tray to provide a clean workspace » Paper towels can be used		

FACIAL TREATMENT PRODUCTS, TOOLS, SUPPLIES AND EQUIPMENT

SUPPLIES	FUNCTION	CLEANING GUIDELINES	DISINFECTION GUIDELINES
Single-Use Gloves	» Protect hands » Prevent cross-contamination » Use non-latex gloves that fit tightly	» Single-use item per client, must be discarded at end of service.	» Cannot be disinfected, discard after one use.
Sheet, Blanket	» Protects facial treatment table » Provides warmth and comfort to client » Use a fitted and flat sheet (twin size) or two flat sheets (queen size) for a spa-wrap table setup (see *Facial Treatment Skills* lesson)	» Remove hair and debris. » Wash in washing machine after each use in hot water.	» Use an approved laundry additive if required by area's regulatory agency. » Dry thoroughly. » Store appropriately, as required by regulatory agency.
Headband or Hairnet	» Protects client's hair from products » Keeps client's hair out of face		
Client Gown	» Covers and allows client to remove clothing (to prevent staining)	» Remove hair and debris. » Wash in washing machine after each use in hot water.	
Towel	» Cushions client's head » Keeps hair protected » Used to remove mask		
Hot Towel	» Softens the horny layer (stratum corneum) of the skin to remove dead skin or blemishes such as milia » Softens the pores to allow for easier removal of comedones and blockages » Improves circulation by encouraging vasodilation causing erythema	» Remove hair and debris. » Wash in washing machine after each use in hot water.	

SUPPLIES	FUNCTION	CLEANING GUIDELINES	DISINFECTION GUIDELINES
Disposable Sponge	» Removes products	» Single-use item, must be discarded.	» Cannot be disinfected, discard after one use.
Distilled Water	» Used in steamer machine » Used in spray machine and Lucas spray pulverizer with specific botanical additives	N/A	N/A
Handheld Mirror	» Allows client to see results	» Clean with 70% alcohol or glass cleaner. » Dry. » Proceed with disinfection.	» After each use, spray with an approved EPA-registered disinfectant solution; let sit for desired contact time, wipe off. » Rinse well. » Dry.

Note: Store disinfected tools and multi-use supplies in a clean, dry, covered container.

INDUSTRY CONNECTION

Using Supplies Wisely

The cost of goods is a large part of expenses in a salon/spa. The supplies used for facials can have a large impact on costs. If you're planning on being self-employed, this is an important area to master. Here are some quick tips to help you control your product usage:

1. Have measuring spoons and cups available to measure recommended amounts of use.
2. Use small bowls for products like serums, eye creams and moisturizers.
3. Dispense the correct amount of disposable supplies into individual containers to use for each facial.
4. Do a complete skin assessment to pull the correct products instead of choosing products as you do the facial.

FACIAL TREATMENT EQUIPMENT

Skin care treatment equipment helps the esthetician perform a thorough and professional analysis and helps cleanse, tone and moisturize the skin. The use of equipment sets the professional facial treatment apart from what clients can do at home.

FACIAL TREATMENT - EQUIPMENT

EQUIPMENT	DESCRIPTION	FUNCTION	INFECTION CONTROL AND SAFETY GUIDELINES
Magnifying Lamp AKA: Loupe	» Allows a thorough analysis of the skin » Can be wall-mounted, attached to a cart or stand independently on a specially designed base	» Provides glare-free light and magnification to determine skin type and condition	» Clean regularly with a soft cloth. » Disinfect with disinfectant at end of each day following manufacturer's instructions; allow to dry. » Remove fingerprints from lens with a cloth dampened with water. » Avoid use of alcohol or solvents on lens. » Check that bulb is secure. » Be aware of electrical cords to avoid accidents.
Wood's Lamp	» Allows for identification of skin type and pigmentation conditions » Identifies skin infection » Uses blacklight	» Identifies areas of oil production on face » Can identify the presence of bacteria	» Clean regularly with a soft cloth. » Disinfect with disinfectant at end of each day following manufacturer's instructions; allow to dry. » Wipe off room-darkening vinyl drape (if applicable) with appropriate disinfectant for the manufacturer's recommended contact time. Rinse, allow to air dry, store according to regulatory guidelines. » Remove fingerprints from lens with a cloth dampened with water. » Avoid use of alcohol or solvents on lens. » Check that bulb is secure. » Be aware of electrical cords to avoid accidents.

EQUIPMENT	DESCRIPTION	FUNCTION	INFECTION CONTROL AND SAFETY GUIDELINES
Steamer	» Skin-warming device used during or following the cleansing process or during an exfoliation treatment » Sprays a hot, diffused vapor mist onto the surface of face using distilled water	» Uses warm, humid mist to expand pores for cleansing » Softens pores to allow easier removal of comedones and blockages » Helps desquamation in skin » Activates certain ingredients such as enzymes	» Wipe down the arms and body of steamer to disinfect after each use according to manufacturer's instructions. » Water level should comply with the manufacturer's instructions. » Adjust ventilating systems to avoid interference with steam flow over the face. » Clean inside steamer each month with distilled water and white vinegar or coffee-pot cleaner to remove and avoid calcium deposits. » Check electrical connections and water levels, pre-heat steamer before use. » After steamer has cooled, empty remaining water from steaming container. » Cleanse glass or plastic steaming container following manufacturer's instructions. » Never allow water to sit in steamer overnight; empty daily. » Use caution around electrical cords.
Hot Towel Cabinet	» Heated cabinet with controllable temperature » Available in variety of sizes according to number and size of towels needed » Some towel cabinets have UV lamps inside to help decrease bacteria; this does not replace appropriate disinfection.	» Keeps warm, damp towels ready to remove products from skin	» Disinfect with appropriate disinfectant at end of day. » Clean out drip tray daily. » Check electrical connections before use. » Turn off at the end of each day. » After towel cabinet has cooled, wipe moisture from cabinet. » Never allow water or towels to sit overnight; empty daily. » Wipe down the outside of machine daily with appropriate disinfectant following manufacturer's instructions and regulatory guidelines.

FACIAL TREATMENT PRODUCTS, TOOLS, SUPPLIES AND EQUIPMENT

EQUIPMENT	DESCRIPTION	FUNCTION	INFECTION CONTROL AND SAFETY GUIDELINES
Treatment Table	» Holds client during facial treatment service	» Provides adjustable height to allow comfortable working surface » Hydraulic or electric is best for ergonomics	» Lock in position before inviting client to lie down. » Wipe down with an approved EPA-registered disinfectant after each use. » Follow basic electrical precautions; ensure loose or frayed wires are repaired.
Cart	» Holds all facial treatment accessories and skin care products	» Keeps everything in order to help with the process of facial	» Disinfect with an approved EPA-registered disinfectant after each use.
Bolster	» Elongated cushion used to support client	» Placed either under client's knees, arms or neck to keep them comfortable during treatment	» Change and wash outer cover after each use. » Can also be covered in disposable treatment table roll that is disposed of after each use.

Always follow appropriate infection control guidelines according to your regulatory agency.

Always follow appropriate infection control guidelines according to your regulatory agency.

Knowing facial treatment products, tools, supplies and equipment helps you provide consistent and measurable results.

LESSONS LEARNED

» The function of products used to perform facial treatments can be identified by reviewing the appropriate charts in this lesson.

» The function of tools and supplies used to perform facial treatments can be identified by reviewing the appropriate charts in this lesson.

» The function of the equipment used to perform facial treatments can be identified by reviewing the appropriate charts in this lesson.

107.3 FACIAL TREATMENT SKILLS

EXPLORE // *Always follow appropriate infection control guidelines according to your regulatory agency.*

Why do you think a facial can cost $35 at one salon/spa and $70 at another?

INSPIRE //

Understanding facial treatment skills will help you offer the most requested service in the salon/spa.

ACHIEVE //

Following this lesson on *Facial Treatment Skills*, you'll be able to:

» State how to drape a client for a facial treatment

» Identify the procedures used to perform a facial treatment

» Describe the guidelines for using facial treatment equipment

FOCUS //

FACIAL TREATMENT SKILLS

Facial Treatment Draping Guidelines

Facial Treatment Procedures

Facial Treatment Equipment Guidelines

Mastering facial treatment skills is one of the most important parts of a successful career in esthetics. Providing a service that meets your client's needs and helps them have a relaxing experience is the key to getting lifelong clients. To do this, there are some key areas to learn:

» Proper facial treatment draping

» Facial treatment procedures

» Proper use of facial treatment equipment

When meeting and greeting clients, you must be at ease, relaxed and ready to assist the client with all their skincare needs. Feeling comfortable with your facial treatment skills will help you achieve this.

FACIAL TREATMENT DRAPING GUIDELINES

Clients will book the initial treatment based on their skin care concerns, but rebook based on how you made them feel. This starts with draping and includes:

» Comfort of the treatment table and draping
» Correct body positioning with bolsters or other positioning aids
» Proper temperature for comfort within the room and on the table
» Environmental setup such as aromatherapy, music, product smell and lighting

For the client's safety and protection, follow proper draping guidelines for all facial services. Be sure to prepare your treatment table before your client arrives.

COCOON WRAP

The cocoon wrap is designed to create a secure and warm environment for your client. It is a simple table setup. Keep in mind, it may be too confining for some clients.

» Place and turn on heated table pad (a table cover or twin fitted sheet over the top is optional)
» Drape queen-size cotton blanket horizontally over treatment table
» Position queen-size white cotton sheet over blanket

» Lay one hand towel across top of table
» Place one folded hand towel at top of the treatment table to wrap client's head

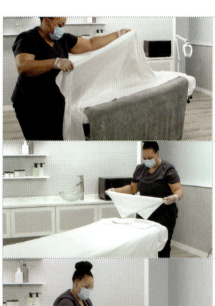

» Have client lay on top of sheet
» Fold one side toward the middle of the client
» Fold back upper corners of sheet, exposing the chest area
» Repeat on opposite side toward middle of the client, while folding back upper corners, exposing the chest area

» Fold the bottom that is hanging down neatly under feet
» Tuck a towel underneath cocoon wrap and then place it up to cover chest area

LAYERED TREATMENT-TABLE SETUP

Another commonly used option for your treatment table is the layered treatment-table setup. This setup is just like making a twin bed. You can pre-make your layered treatment table in preparation for the client; once the client is draped, you can assist them onto the treatment table.

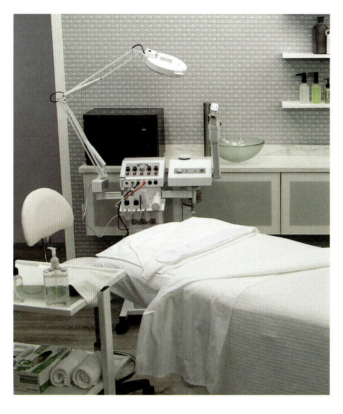

- » Place and turn on heated table pad
- » Drape a twin fitted sheet over the top of the table pad
- » Lay one flat body towel horizontally across top of table

- » Place one folded hand towel at the top of the treatment table to wrap client's head
- » Lay twin sheet over the top of the treatment table

- » Put a twin duvet, blanket or comforter over the top of the sheet
- » Fold sheet top down over duvet, blanket or comforter

Assist the client onto the table, then pull the sheet, duvet, blanket or comforter completely over the client and make any last-minute adjustments, such as adding extra bolsters, pillows or towels, adjusting the warmth of the treatment table, and putting on more or taking off blankets.

Tip: If you are working on a male or a large person, the layered treatment table setup is more comfortable.

HEAD WRAP

Use the folded towel at the top of the table (indicated in both draping methods) for draping a client's head as well as to protect the hair from product.

- » Fold hand towel with both ends pointing toward head of treatment table
- » Place adjustable headband along the straight end of folded towel

- » Place under client's head at base of skull (occipital)
- » Fold up and secure at top of forehead

Note: If your client has long hair, a hairnet or additional towel may be used to protect it.

FACIAL TREATMENT DRAPING CONSIDERATIONS

Every client is unique, and some may have special challenges or preferences that need to be taken into consideration when getting a facial treatment, and draping will be adjusted to suit their needs. These considerations might include:

- Pregnancy
- Disability
- Age
- Gender
- Body size
- Comfort preference (temperature)

Here are some general tips for working with draping considerations:

Pregnancy	» Support the client with bolsters and pillows » Adjust the temperature of the room to their comfort » Allow more time for the preparation and completion of the treatment » Use a hydraulic or electric treatment table and lower for easy access **Note:** During the client's second trimester, when placed in the supine (upward-facing) position, it puts pressure on the subclavian vein, which could cause complications. Use caution and make sure your client is aware of risks.
Disability	The U.S. and Canada both have disability requirements. Be sure to follow the laws for your area. In general: » Allow space in the treatment room for wheelchairs, walkers or other assistive devices » Remove potential hazards (remove any rugs or cords that could hamper access) » Allow more time for the client getting on and off the treatment table » Support client with bolsters and pillows » Allow more time for the preparation and completion of the treatment » Use a hydraulic or electric treatment table and lower for easy access

Minor Clients	» Have space for a chaperone to sit while ensuring the area is safe from hazards
Elderly Clients	» Support the client with bolsters and pillows where appropriate » Allow more time for the preparation and completion of the treatment » Use a hydraulic or electric treatment table and lower for easy access
Male Clients	» Support client with bolsters and pillows where appropriate » Use larger-size sheets, duvet, blankets or comforters
Body Size (Large Clients)	» Support the client with bolsters and pillows where appropriate » Allow more time for the preparation and completion of the treatment » Use a hydraulic or electric treatment table and lower for easy access » Use larger-size sheets, duvet, blankets or comforters

Note: Keep in mind clients of all ages can experience temperature fluctuations. This tends to make the client warmer or cooler in the treatment room, and they may experience several changes between temperatures during the facial. Watch their body language and and be ready to make any draping adjustments that the client needs.

When a client enters the treatment room, be sure to advise the client on how to disrobe and where to lie down. It can be embarrassing for the client if they don't know what to do, and this could influence the client's decision on whether to return for a follow-up treatment or not.

Each client is different, and occasionally there are unique factors to consider. Being prepared for all eventualities will make life easier for both the client and esthetician.

FACIAL TREATMENT PROCEDURES

The facial treatment, which is typically an hour long, follows all the procedures presented in this lesson. However, it can be modified by products or specialized with techniques implemented by skin care companies.

Developing your technical skills and following systematic procedures will allow you to achieve accuracy and consistency in all your work. The facial treatment procedures include:

INCREASE PHASE

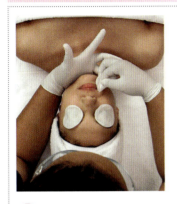
1. Pre-Cleanse

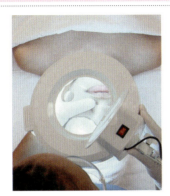
2. Analyze

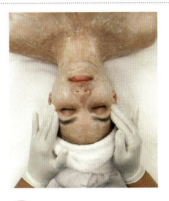
3. Cleanse and Tone

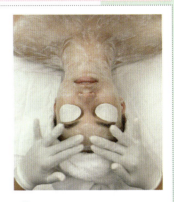
4. Exfoliate

BALANCE PHASE

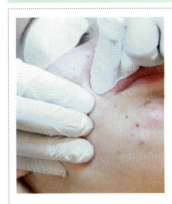
5. Treat

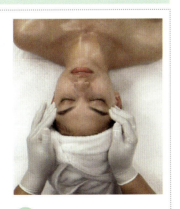
6. Massage

DECREASE PHASE

7. Mask

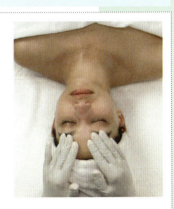
8. Protect

Each of these steps can be modified for services such as express facial treatments, acne facial treatments, or men's facial treatments. Knowing the basic facial treatment, will help you understand the other facial workshops.

◉ FACIAL TREATMENT – PRE-CLEANSE

The Pre-Cleanse removes all makeup that the client is wearing. If no makeup is present, this process is still performed to ensure you remove all surface debris. Also known as "superficial cleanse" or "first cleanse," this is the initial step of any facial, and it allows you to make a comprehensive analysis of the skin. You'll treat the eyes and lips first with a product specific to those areas. Then the upper chest, neck and face are cleansed using cleansing application movements light pressure and fast rhythm.

PRE-CLEANSE STEP

 Goal: To start cleansing the skin and stimulate microcirculation. Prepare for skin analysis. This is performed with every facial treatment service.

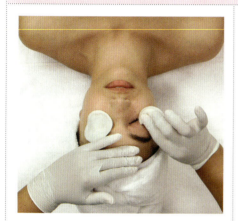

Wash hands and apply single-use gloves and any additional PPE required by your regulatory agency.

Drape/cover client appropriately.

Place cotton pads saturated with makeup remover on each eye.
- » Use light circular movements to help dissolve eye makeup.

Remove lipstick:
- » Hold outer corner of mouth and wipe twice toward center of lips.
- » Hold outer corner of mouth and wipe once to other side of lips.
- » Take second saturated pad and repeat same steps in other direction.

Remove eye makeup using saturated cotton pads:
- » Fold cotton pad in half; perform downward and inward strokes.
- » Fold new saturated cotton pad in half; have client look upward.
- » Remove eye makeup along lower lashline.

Remove face makeup using a general makeup remover suitable for all skin types. Apply with hands, fan brush or gauze; remove with warm, wet gauze:
- » Work in upward movements from the upper chest; use inward and upward movements over the neck and face.

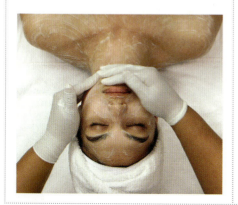

Perform superficial cleanse (first cleanse):
- » Obtain cleanser suitable for all skin types.
- » Use hands to apply cleanser evenly over upper chest, neck and face.
- » Use cleansing application movements with light pressure and fast rhythm.

Remove cleanser with wet gauze; discard after use.

◉ FACIAL TREATMENT – ANALYZE

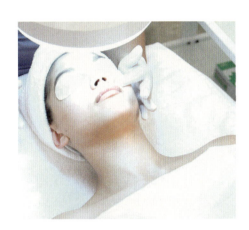

As you learned in the *Skin* area of study, skin analysis is one of the most important parts of a facial treatment. In this step, you will be using the Skin Assessment and Recommendation System, which includes identifying:

» Any skin conditions and possible contraindications for treatment
» Your client's skin type
» Your client's Fitzpatrick skin type

This allows you to choose the correct products, tools and devices to incorporate into your facial protocol. This step of the facial also helps you determine the home care products to recommend at the end of the facial.

ANALYZE STEP

 Goal: To correctly identify skin type, skin condition, Fitzpatrick skin type. Identify contraindications and cautions for treatment, correct products for safe service results. This is performed with every facial treatment service.

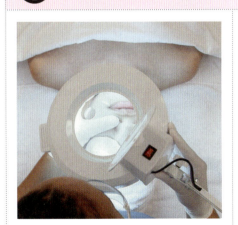

Identify contraindications and cautions

Identify skin type and Fitzpatrick type:
» Apply eye pads
» Place magnifying lamp 2-3" (5-7.5 cm) from face

Note: Distance may vary based on strength of magnification, client's skin and your eye sight
» Use skin charting form

Use Wood's lamp as directed in the skin assessment system

Identify skin condition categories:
» Use "Look, Ask, Touch" guidelines

Create summary analysis:
» Determine products and tools to use for Increase, Balance and Decrease results
» Notate findings on skin charting form summary area
» Identify treatment to perform and any modifications
» Discuss treatment plan and obtain consent from client

🌀 FACIAL TREATMENT – CLEANSE AND TONE

Next is the Cleanse and Tone step of the facial. After you have done your skin assessment and identified the best products to use for results, you will perform the second cleanse. This is done with cleansing application movements using medium-slow rhythm and pressure.

This cleanse is referred to as the second cleanse because it is done after the pre-cleanse (or first cleanse) that happens before the Analyze step.

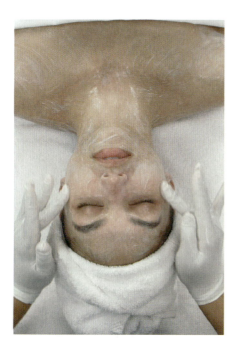

Cleanse
- » Performed with specific cleanser for client's skin type
  - » Slightly longer than first cleanse with slower movements and medium pressure
  - » Equipment such as a brush machine can be used in this step; you will learn more in the *Facial Treatments With Devices* area of study.

Tone
- » Helps remove any residual cleansing product
- » Rebalances pH of skin

Note: Blot-dry excess toner immediately to remove excess moisture.

CLEANSE AND TONE STEP

 Goal: To deep cleanse the skin and continue stimulation of microcirculation. This is performed with most facial treatments; toner is omitted for chemical exfoliation services at this step.

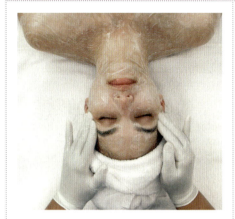

Apply cleanser evenly over upper chest, neck and face (second cleanse):
- Use smooth, sweeping effleurage strokes.
- Be consistent; remain in contact with face until cleansing is complete.

Note: If using a gel cleanser, emulsify (dampen your fingers in your bowl, mix gel cleanser with damp hands or whip with a fan brush) first, then apply.

Perform cleansing application movements:
- Use both hands
- Use medium-slow movements with medium pressure
- Work upward from upper chest
- Use gliding effleurage movements:
    - Begin at center of chest, move across chest then upward on neck
    - Center of chin then to jawline
    - Jawline to corner of mouth
    - Across cheeks to temple
    - Temple to nose, side of nose, up to forehead
    - Across forehead returning to temples
    - Use two fingers to work under eyes toward bridge of nose and out over eyelid
    - Slide down outer portion of face to chest

Repeat effleurage movements up to three times:
- Use circular movements:
    - Across chest and up neck
    - From center of chin to jawline
    - Jawline to corner of mouth
    - Across cheeks then back to nose
    - Up both sides of nose
    - Up to forehead
    - Across forehead to temples
    - Circle down the temples to the eyes
    - Circle eyes along orbital bone
    - Slide down outer side of face back to chest area then slide off in preparation of next step
- Repeat circular movements up to three times.

Remove cleanser using a steamed towel or warm, wet gauze:
- Begin at upper chest; open towel and wrap face
- Remove cleanser from face, neck and upper chest
- Avoid dragging or pulling skin
- Follow procedure until all cleanser has been removed

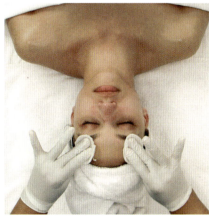

Apply toner to skin with a cotton pad:
- Begin at upper chest; open towel and wrap face
- Remove cleanser from face, neck , upper chest
- Use a sweeping movement
- Blot off excess moisture with a tissue

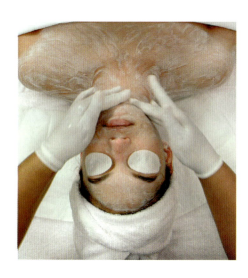

FACIAL TREATMENT – EXFOLIATE

Exfoliation helps remove the top layers of the stratum corneum, which aids in the absorption of the products used in the facial. This process also allows for deeper cleansing of the pores and encourages cellular renewal. Exfoliating the skin can be adapted to suit all skin types and conditions, depending on the product and how it is applied.

As you learned in the *Skin Theory* lesson, there are two classifications of exfoliation: mechanical and chemical. Each type has a purpose and can be used for specific effects. For example, the use of an enzyme exfoliant is gentle enough for most skin conditions. As you gain experience, you will be able to adapt your protocols to address all issues. You will learn more about chemical exfoliation in the *Chemical Exfoliation* lesson.

If using an enzyme exfoliant instead of a granular scrub, apply as a mask with steam or follow the specific manufacturer's instructions.

EXFOLIATE STEP

 Goal: To continue increased microcirculation, stimulate cell turnover and improve skin texture. This is performed for all facial treatments.

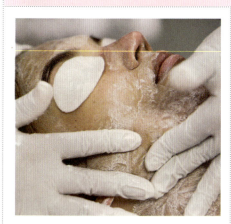

Turn on steamer:
- Position behind the client's head or to the side.

Note: Do not use a steam application if it is contraindicated on the client's skin charting, e.g., sensitive skin types.

Apply granular exfoliant to client's skin:
- Dispense scrub in small bowl.
- Warm the product in your hand and apply to the skin.
- Begin at chest and work upward to neck and face.
- Avoid eyelids and mouth.
- Massage in circular movements until slight erythema (mild redness) occurs.
- Steam for 5-10 minutes.
- Position 12-18" (30-45 cm) from face.
- Always follow manufacturer's instructions.

Note: Do not use a granular exfoliant on sensitive skin or acne.

Remove exfoliant using warm steam towel wrap:
- Release the steam to avoid discomfort or burning.
- Test the temperature on your wrist.
- Wrap face with steam towel, gently press down on face and forehead.
- Leave on until product is moist.
- Wipe downward from forehead to jaw on each side of face.
- Wipe across chest and up neck with towel.
- May need to use more towels or warm, wet gauze to remove excess. Be certain all exfoliant is removed from skin before moving forward with next step.

Note: A tissue or paper towel may be added under the client's head to catch scrub that may fall off.

FACIAL TREATMENT – TREAT

The Treat step of the facial is designed to treat skin conditions by using specialized serums, devices and/or extraction of impurities, if indicated. These products are chosen after a thorough skin assessment. This step of the facial can be interchanged with massage, based on whether or not extraction is performed.

Extractions should be performed if the skin is clogged with oil and impurities. Once the sebum is softened within the skin from the steaming, gentle extractions will assist in removing blackheads out of the follicle. Often, massage is put first before an extraction to avoid spreading bacteria.

This is performed for most facial treatments. It can be omitted for express facials and chemical exfoliation.

TREAT STEP

 Goal: To infuse active ingredients in the skin, address specific skin conditions. This is performed as needed with most facial treatments.

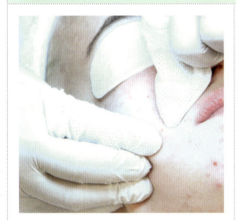

Perform extractions on comedones using finger-extraction method:

- Apply eye pads.
- Apply a thin layer of desincrustation solution and steam for 3 minutes.
- Position magnifying lamp over face so you can see clearly; however, no closer than 1-2" (2.5-5cm).
- Wrap gauze pads moistened with astringent or desincrustation solution around index fingers.
- Place index finger on each side of the comedone.
- Press down around the comedone.
- Lift skin under the comedone and gently compress skin, moving slightly back-and-forth in a rocking motion.
- Immediately blot with astringent to kill bacteria.
- Do not force sebum out of skin; be gentle.
- Do not use fingernails or other sharp instruments.
- Do not perform extraction for more than 5 minutes.

Note: Cotton swabs can be used instead of fingers wrapped in gauze.

Apply treatment serum:

- Choose serum based on client's skin condition.
- Always follow manufacturer's instructions.
- Dispense product into small container.
- Apply serum with fan brush in upward strokes from chest to forehead.
- Gently massage product into skin using large, circular, effleurage movements until serum is absorbed.

Always follow appropriate infection control guidelines according to your regulatory agency.

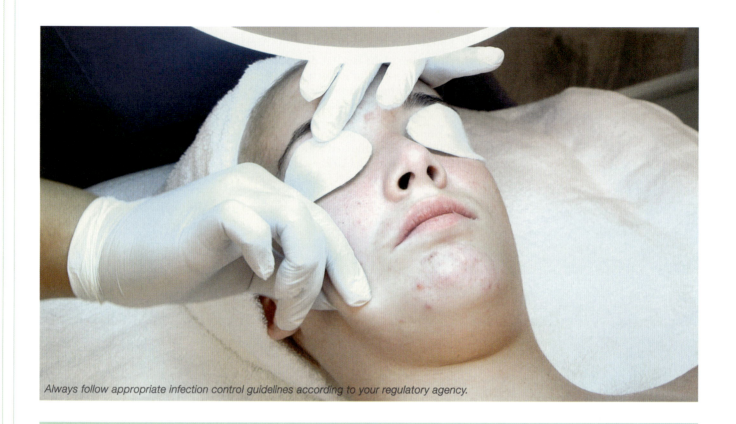
Always follow appropriate infection control guidelines according to your regulatory agency.

DISCOVER MORE

Dr. Jacquet Movements

Dr. Jacquet movements are for loosening and expelling excess sebum from the follicle. The movement is used for oily and acne-blemished skin.

Once the skin has been warmed with steam, enabling the pores to dilate, the sebum is softened and can be removed from the pores with a gentle method of extraction. The skin can be easily bruised if you apply too much pressure. Be careful and communicate with the client to ensure there is not too much discomfort.

Dr. Jacquet massage movement:

» After the skin is cleansed, steamed and exfoliated

» Grasp a small section of skin between the thumb and forefinger and squeeze gently, while twisting or kneading; this movement will simulate a snapping motion but with small sections of skin in between your fingers

» Use petrissage movements in small sections around the face, if needed

» Proceed with extraction

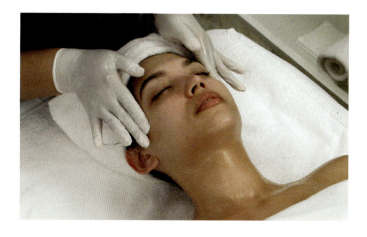
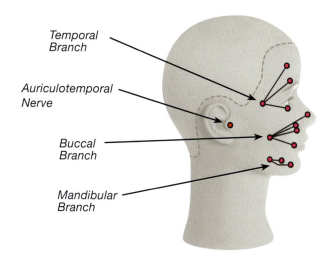

⊙ FACIAL TREATMENT – MASSAGE

Massage is one of the most important skills to develop. **Massage** is a systematic, therapeutic method of manipulating the body by rubbing, pinching, tapping, kneading or stroking with hands, fingers or an instrument. It occurs with all facial treatments, except for treatments that are highly stimulating to the skin, such as chemical exfoliation and microdermabrasion.

The **origin** of the muscle is the immoveable part, while the **insertion** is the part of the muscle that moves. Massage movements designed to stimulate the muscle directly should be done from the insertion to the origin of the muscle. This is to avoid damage to muscle tissues that can happen with too much pressure.

Muscle does not attach directly to the dermis, rather to the hypodermis (see the *Skin Theory* lesson). Therefore, some movements designed to stimulate the skin lightly may not be in the insertion-to-origin direction. Those movements should be done lightly, toward the heart or lymph nodes.

Massage is a skill that gets better with experience. To start mastering this skill, it is important to understand:

- Massage benefits
- The five basic massage movements
- Massage procedure
- Massage guidelines

Once the basics are understood, you will find that creating your own signature massage routines will become easy.

MASSAGE BENEFITS

Massage has multiple benefits to the skin and body. Massage increases circulation to help remove waste from body cells at a more efficient rate. Increased circulation and renewed flexibility are two major benefits. In addition to the physical benefits, it is also emotionally soothing, since the human body responds well to touch that is safe, caring and confident.

Massage improves lymphatic drainage and blood flow. These effects can greatly improve the skin's texture, tone and color. Specialized techniques and movements can be added to achieve more benefits and effects.

The ability to deliver a relaxing, satisfactory massage is one benefit that clients cannot achieve at home, and is an excellent method for providing a restful, relaxing skin care treatment to a client. Every muscle and nerve has a motor point. The main motor points that are involved in a facial massage include:

- Temporal branch
- Auriculotemporal branch
- Buccal branch
- Mandibular branch

Applying pressure to these motor points soothes and stimulates the nerves and muscles (see illustration).

Benefits of massage include:

- Increases circulation of the blood supply to the skin, causing blood vessels to dilate
- Stimulates the glandular activities of the skin
- Helps stimulate weak muscle
- Temporarily relieves pain
- Softens and improves the texture and complexion
- Calms and relaxes the client
- Relieves emotional stress and body tension

This is performed for most facial treatments, but can be omitted for express facials and stimulating facial treatments like chemical exfoliation.

FACIAL TREATMENT SKILLS

THE FIVE BASIC MOVEMENTS OF MASSAGE

Each massage movement performs a different benefit and delivers specific effects. Basic movements have specific techniques that can be used to provide optimal results. You will often see movements referred to as the technique name, such as "hand-over-hand" or "large circles." The direction, depth of pressure and speed all play a role in how your movements affect your client. Be sure to check your ergonomics to keep your hands, arms and shoulders safe.

This step is yet another area in the facial service that can be adapted according to skin conditions. Additional training will help you adapt these basic movements.

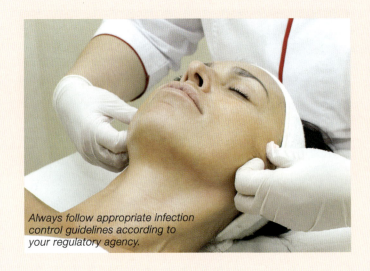

Always follow appropriate infection control guidelines according to your regulatory agency.

BASIC MOVEMENT DESCRIPTION		HOW TO	BENEFITS AND EFFECTS	PURPOSE
	EFFLEURAGE (EF-loo-rahzh) **Movement Name:** » Hand over hand » Slide (sweeping) » Small circles » Large circles » 4-finger interlock glide A light, rhythmic, continuous stroking or circular movement. Means "to skim" in French.	» Use palms of hands and pads of fingers » Both hands used at the same time or alternating hands » Begin with light pressure then adjust as needed » Use consistent pressure in the upward stroke » Use light pressure on the downward stroke	» Increases desquamation » Soothes the nervous system » Increases circulation and lymphatic flow » Relaxes contracted tense muscle fibers » Introduces the esthetician's hands by applying the massage medium	» Relax client » Product application » Cleansing movements » Movement Transitions
	PETRISSAGE (PAY-tre-sahzh) **Movement Name:** » Finger-twist pinch » Thumb kneading » Rolling and pinching » Pull up and hold A light or heavy kneading and rolling of the muscles. It is used on the face, the arms, the shoulders and the upper back. Means "to knead" in French.	» Lift and compress the muscles between the thumb and fingers » For larger muscles press the palm of the hand firmly over the muscles, then grasp and lift with the heel of the hand and the fingers » Use consistent pressure in the upward and downward movements	» Provides deep stimulation of muscles and nerves » Improves muscle tone » Increases sebaceous and sudoriferous gland activity » Increases circulation and lymphatic flow » Probably the most important of the massage movements due to its beneficial effects.	» Stimulate circulation » Increase gland activity to help dry skin » Sensitive skin stimulation without erythema

BASIC MOVEMENT DESCRIPTION (CONT'D)	HOW TO	BENEFITS AND EFFECTS	PURPOSE
PERCUSSION (per-**CUSS**-shun) (**TAPOTEMENT**) **Movement Name:** » Tapping » Windmill Also known as **tapotement**, is a light tapping or slapping movement applied with the fingertips or partly flexed fingers. The movement is usually carried out on the body with the hands swinging freely from the wrist in a rapid motion.	» Use pads of fingers to quickly tap across skin » Use palms of both hands to perform fast hand-over-hand movements upward from chest, neck and under jaw Hacking is a form of tapotement that is like a chopping movement with the edge of the hands; used on the arms, back and shoulders.	» Stimulates nerves » Increases blood circulation » Promotes muscle contraction » Do not use when the client needs soothing	» Tones skin » Treats aging skin
FRICTION **Movement Name:** » Scissor » Half circles A circular or wringing movement that moves skin over underlying structures with no gliding, usually carried out with the fingertips or palms of the hands.	» Use pads of fingers and both hands » Use medium pressure » Use a fast rhythm » Cross fingers in scissor movement or half circles Friction is used most often on the scalp, hands or with less pressure during a facial massage.	» Stimulates nerves » Increases desquamation » Improves scar tissue and adhesions » Improves circulation » Relaxes trigger points (tight nodules in muscle fiber)	» Relieves stress » Relaxes muscle tension » Acne treatments » Scalp massage » Hand and arm massage
VIBRATION **Movement Name:** » Vibrations » Slapping A shaking movement in the arms of the esthetician, while the fingertips or palms are touching the client.	Vibration should only be used in facial massage for a few seconds in one location, as it is very stimulating to the skin.	» Stimulates nerves » Improves skin function	» Sensitive skin stimulation without erythema

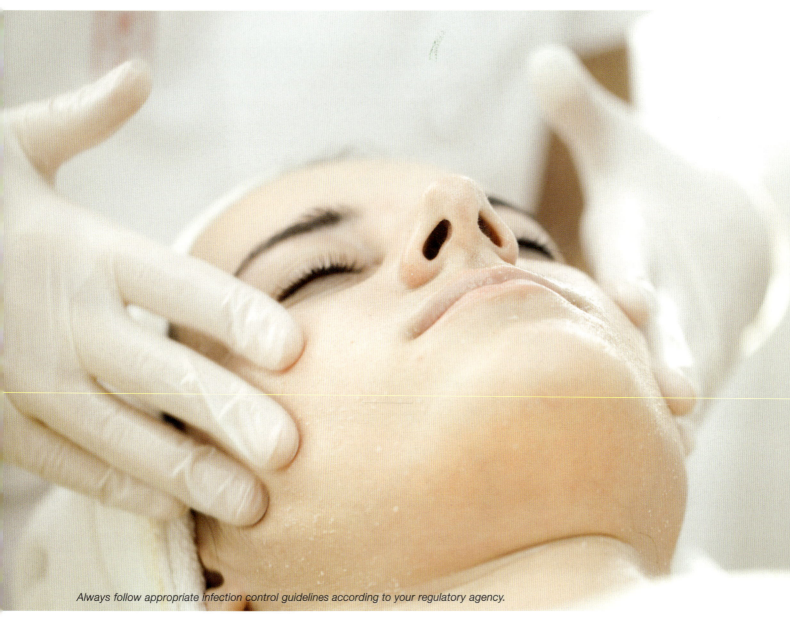

Always follow appropriate infection control guidelines according to your regulatory agency.

To avoid discomfort or possible injury, pressure must not be applied over bony areas, the carotid artery, the sternocleidomastoid muscle or trachea.

When you massage skin that is prone to redness or erythema, consider using light massage strokes. The use of a very stimulating massage is not an option for skin in this condition.

MASSAGE PROCEDURES

The massage procedure used in a facial treatment should not exceed 15 minutes and incorporates all five massage movements:

- » Apply massage medium using product application movements:
  - » Remove client's eye pads
  - » Choose massage medium based on skin type and condition
  - » Obtain with clean spatula
  - » Apply to both hands
- » Perform massage movements using slow rhythm and light pressure:
  - » Face
  - » Neck
  - » Upper chest
  - » Shoulders

FACIAL TREATMENT – BASIC MASSAGE STEPS

Goal: To continue infusing active ingredients into the skin, help improve hydration, improve texture and reduce inflammation. This is performed for most facial treatments excluding services with grade 3 acne or higher.

1. Place fingertips of both hands at top of sternum, have client take a deep breath.

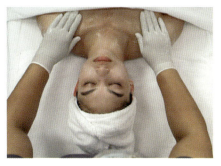

2. Perform large circle movements using both hands across upper chest, around shoulder and up trapezius.

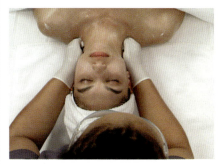

3. Perform thumb-kneading movements with both hands on both sides of posterior neck to occipital.

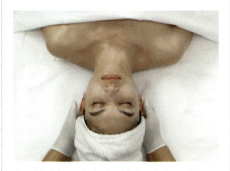

4. Hold occipital with both hands and gently stretch neck for 10 seconds, then slide hands to upper chest.

Note: If the client has a neck injury, omit this step.

5. Work to the shoulders, then using thumb-kneading movements, move along the trapezius working up the neck.

6. Slide hands back to upper chest.

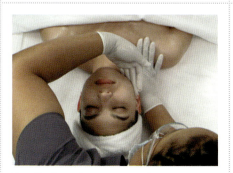

7. Perform **long, sweeping** hand-over-hand movements from the upper chest to jawline. Repeat twice.

8. Slide both hands to base of skull.

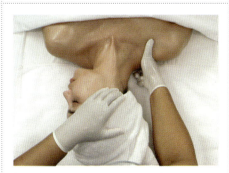

9. Using both hands, gently turn the client's head to the side and use large circular kneading movements up the trapezius, then the sternocleidomastoid, ending at the ear. Slide back to base of skull.

BASIC MASSAGE STEPS (CONT'D)

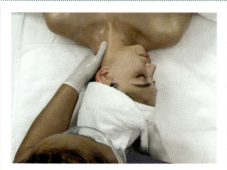

10. Repeat on other side, then slide both hands back to upper chest.

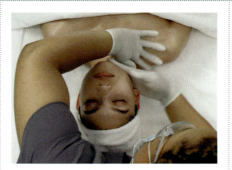

11. Perform fast windmill movements with both hands and move up the neck. Move across the jawline both directions, then stop on chin. Repeat twice.

12. Apply pressure at center of chin.

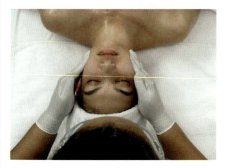

13. Perform small circular movements with both hands back-and-forth along jawline, ending at corners of mouth.

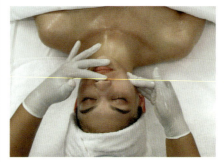

14. Perform scissor movements with alternating hands on mouth and chin. Repeat twice.

15. Slide to cheeks, then perform pull-up-and-hold movement on cheeks with both hands, then slide to chin.

16. Perform small circular movements with fingertips of both hands, beginning at chin, working up toward forehead.

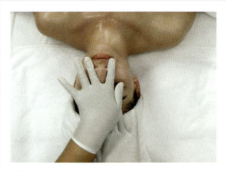

17. Slide to corrugator, then perform scissor movements with alternating hands upward on nose, then slide down sides of nose.

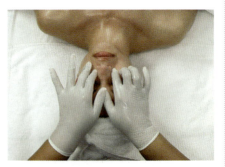

18. Perform small circular movements at outer corner of nose, move up side of nose around eyes and back to nose.

BASIC MASSAGE STEPS (CONT'D)

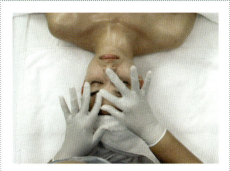

19. Perform figure-eight movement around eyes, repeat six times, then slide to temple.

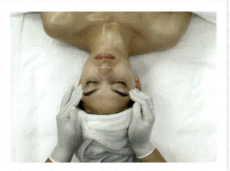

20. Perform small circular movements around temple with both hands, then pause at temples and apply pressure.

21. Perform a tapping movement around eyes, move in a circle outside of eyes with ring and index fingers.

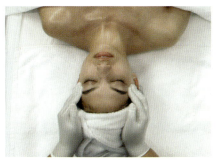

22. Slide to temples, perform a pressure point movement, then slide the right hand over to the left.

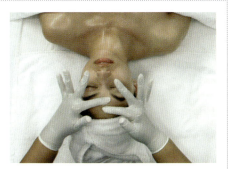

23. Perform half-circle movements back and forth across forehead. Repeat.

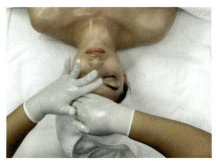

24. Perform a sweeping hand-over-hand movement beginning at forehead. Repeat.

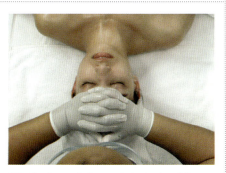

25. Perform 4-finger interlock glide movement on forehead. Repeat twice.

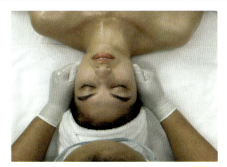

26. Slide down sides of face to earlobes and gently pull off.

FACIAL TREATMENT MASSAGE GUIDELINES

- Always check for contraindications first since massage increases circulation and could present a risk for some clients.
- Avoid removing your hands from the client's face once massage movement has begun and never remove them abruptly. Making and breaking contact with the skin in the same manner over time enables the client to become expectant of the process and comfortable with it.
- Massage should never be uncomfortable for the client. Pressure that is too deep or aggressive should be avoided. Watch for non-verbal clues for discomfort and verbally check with your client.
- Know all the underlying structures you are working on, such as the location of the neck veins and arteries. This enables you to avoid applying too much pressure.
- Provide even rhythm and pressure when performing facial movements to ensure a relaxing effect.

Other Massage Techniques

One of the exciting things about massage is the number of advanced techniques and protocols you can learn to add to your skills. Mastering the theory and basic movements of massage lays the foundation for you to get additional training. Other massage techniques you may learn about include:

Shiatsu	Shiatsu is a form of Japanese bodywork based on concepts in traditional Chinese medicine. Shiatsu derives from a Japanese massage modality called Anma. It uses acupressure points to relax and balance the body.
Acupressure	Acupressure massage is an ancient remedy of Chinese traditional medicine known to relieve pain in specific areas of the body. It consists of applying pressure to specific points of the face and body to release muscular tension, stimulate and restore balance (Chi). Acupressure is often the choice for people who prefer a natural form of pain relief instead of using medication.
Manual Lymph Drainage (MLD)	MLD is a light-pressure massage for the lymphatic system to remove waste from the body. Helps with edema, erythema, puffiness, discoloration under the eyes, acne and cellulite.
Aromatherapy Massage	Aromatherapy allows you to combine your chosen massage technique, usually classical massage, with massage oil scented with essential oils that contain certain benefits for the body, mind, spirit.
Scalp Massage	Scalp massage is a relaxing addition to any treatment. Massage by moving the pads of your fingers in a circular motion, start at the base of the scalp (occipital bone), massage to the top of the head, and make sure you have covered the entire scalp for approximately 5-10 minutes. » Massaging the head helps to increase circulation in the scalp. » Increased circulation amplifies the amount of red blood cells in the scalp. » More red blood cells enhance growth and rejuvenation and allow the scalp to produce more hair follicles. » Scalp massage helps to increase the amount of hair growth each month. » Essential oils can be added to a scalp massage treatment.

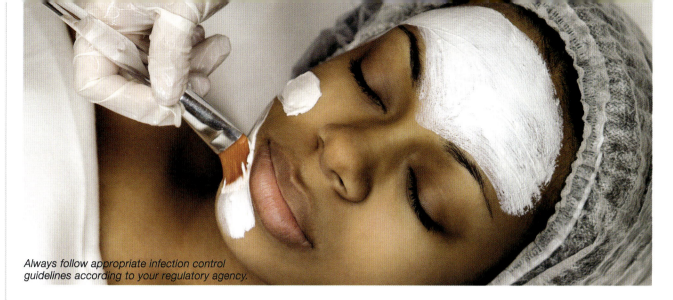

Always follow appropriate infection control guidelines according to your regulatory agency.

FACIAL TREATMENT – MASK

The Mask step of the facial treatment is the start of the Decrease phase. Active ingredients have already been delivered to the skin, and stimulation of microcirculation has been performed. Now you will start to calm and hydrate the skin. Your client should not leave your treatment room highly inflamed and red. Mild erythema is acceptable if extraction or more aggressive treatment has been done, but every effort to calm the skin must be made.

MASK STEP

Goal: To calm, hydrate and reduce inflammation. This is performed for all facial treatments.

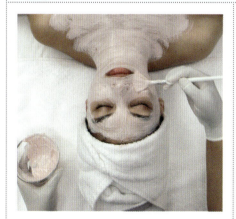

Apply mask using a fan brush with long, sweeping strokes:
- Begin at upper chest and work upward toward the forehead.
- Cover the entire area, including the upper lip.
- Re-apply eye pads.
- Allow mask to set 5-10 minutes or according to manufacturer's instructions.

Tip: Multiple masks can be used. For example, for combination skin, apply a non-setting mask to face, omitting the T-zone, then apply a setting mask (clay) instead.

Remove mask with warm, steamed towel:
- Obtain two towels from hot cabinet.
- Release steam from towels.
- Test temperature of towels before applying.
- Apply one towel across chest.
- Apply second towel. Wrap around face, up around the eyes and forehead.
- Do not cover nostrils.
- Gently press down on chest, face and forehead.
- Leave on for 1 minute.
- Wipe away mask, working from the forehead to jaw, using face towel.
- Wipe across chest and up neck with towel on chest.

Note: Be certain all masking product is removed before moving forward.

Apply toner to skin with cotton or gauze pad:
- Begin at upper chest and work toward forehead.

FACIAL TREATMENT – PROTECT

The Protect step continues the Decrease phase of the facial treatment. It includes the application of serums, eye cream, moisturizer and SPF at end of facial. The products you choose should help calm the skin if needed. This part of the facial treatment can use the same products that will be recommended for home use as well.

At the end of the facial treatment, the skin needs to be left calmed, moisturized and well protected. Application is performed in light, sweeping effleurage movements. Products should always be applied thinnest to thickest; serums, gels, moisturizer, SPF.

PROTECT STEP

Goal: To continue calming, improve hydration, skin barrier function and apply products that may be used in home-care regimens. This is performed for all facial treatments.

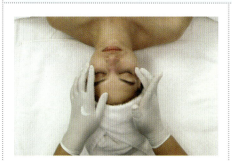

Apply eye cream:
- Dispense small amount into dish.
- Apply with pads of fingers.
- Use small tapping motions around eyes.

Note: Light, circular movements around eyes may be used.

Apply serum, moisturizer and sun protection over upper chest, neck and face:
- Apply with product application movements with light pressure
- Use an SPF 30 or higher

INDUSTRY CONNECTION

Mini-Treatments

One of the latest trends in salon/spas is to offer mini-treatments. The idea is to provide mini versions of the most popular treatments so clients can experience the benefits of the treatments quickly. Generally, the mini-treatments range from 12-30 minutes. They include treatments such as scalp massage, shoulder massage or hand exfoliation and moisturizing. The mini-treatments are also great to add on to expand a one-hour treatment.

Giving clients an opportunity to feel the benefits of a skin care treatment in a short amount of time can easily lead to scheduling full-service treatments later.

FACIAL TREATMENT EQUIPMENT GUIDELINES

Understanding how to safely use facial treatment equipment is an important skill to learn. You will start with:

- Wood's lamp
- Magnifying lamp
- Steamer
- Hot towel cabinet

These are considered basic or essential equipment for a 60-minute facial treatment. Additional esthetics devices are covered in the *Facial Treatments With Devices* area of study. Troubleshooting and client considerations will be covered in the *Facial Treatment Guest Experience* lesson.

GUIDELINES FOR USE

Wood's Lamp

- Use after face is cleansed
- Apply eye pads
- Use in fully dark room or with darkening sleeve
- Hold 2-4" (5-10 cm) above face and move across skin as needed
- Do not touch skin with lamp
- Turn off after use

See the *Skin Analysis* lesson for Wood's lamp results.

Magnifying Lamp

- Loosen the adjustment arm to adjust the lamp up or down
- Adjust the lamp appropriately to avoid overreaching
- Apply eye pads
- Place lamp appropriate distance from client's face for ideal magnification
- Switch the lamp on and position it over the client's face

See the *Skin Analysis* lesson for more information.

Steamer

- Make sure steam cup is filled with distilled water
- Turn on steamer away from client's face
- Cover eyes
- Place behind head at a slight angle
- Use at 12-18" (30-45 cm) from face
- Use for recommended amount of time–usually 10 minutes.
- Move steamer arm away from face
- Turn off

If using the ozone light, turn on after steam has begun and turn off before turning steamer off.

Hot Towel Cabinet

- Turn on towel cabinet
- Apply single-use gloves
- Fold towel in half
- Roll up towel
- Place rolled towel in sink with hot water or in large bowl
- Make sure towels are saturated
- Ring out excess water
- Place towels in towel cabinet
- Turn off at the end of the day
- Remove any excess towels

107E.3 | FACIAL TREATMENT SKILLS

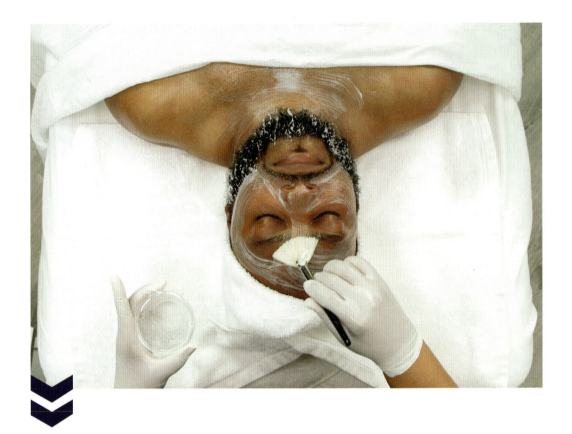

Understanding the facial treatment skills will prepare you to offer the most requested service in the salon/spa.

LESSONS LEARNED

Facial treatment draping guidelines include:

- Cocoon wrap
- Layered treatment-table setup
- Head wrap

Facial treatment procedures (steps) include:

- Pre-Cleanse
- Analyze
- Cleanse and Tone
- Exfoliate
- Treat
- Massage
- Mask
- Protect

Guidelines for using facial treatment equipment include:

- Magnifying lamp
- Wood's lamp
- Steamer
- Hot towel cabinet

107E.4 FACIAL TREATMENT GUEST EXPERIENCE

EXPLORE //

How would you describe the feeling of being pampered?

INSPIRE //

Giving clients the self-assurance that comes with beautiful, healthy skin is rewarding.

ACHIEVE //

Following this lesson on *Facial Treatment Guest Experience*, you'll be able to:

» Identify the service essentials related to facial treatments

» Describe preparation and setup for the facial treatment room

» Explain facial treatment care and safety guidelines

» Provide examples of guidelines to ensure client comfort and satisfaction when performing a facial treatment service

» Summarize the three areas of a facial treatment service

FOCUS //

FACIAL TREATMENT GUEST EXPERIENCE

Facial Treatment Service Essentials

Facial Treatment Room Guidelines

Facial Treatment Care and Safety Guidelines

Facial Treatment Service Client Guidelines

Facial Treatment: Overviews and Rubrics

Your client's experience during a facial is as important as how you perform the service. To some, a facial treatment is a luxurious pamper session. For others, it's an integral part of their health and well-being. You can establish trust and loyalty by creating the perfect facial treatment experience. Make your client's experience enjoyable from beginning to end. If they feel understood, respected and that their needs are always met, this will ensure a long professional relationship.

FACIAL TREATMENT SERVICE ESSENTIALS

Honesty and setting realistic treatment goals go a long way when building relationships. When dealing with clients and their skin care concerns, use empathy and good interpersonal skills.

As with all professional services, consult with your client before the service starts to ensure predictable results and help avoid misunderstandings. Review the four Service Essentials (4 Cs) and how the Skin Assessment and Recommendation System applies to the facial treatment using active listening, critical thinking and analysis.

THE FOUR SERVICE ESSENTIALS (4 Cs)

1. **Connect**
   Establishes rapport and builds credibility with each client
   - Prepare for client
   - Preview client record if available
   - Review client intake form for first-time clients

2. **Consult**
   Analyzes client wants and needs, visualizes the end result, organizes the plan for follow-through and obtains client consent
   - Observe and Analyze steps

3. **Create**
   Produces functional, predictable and pleasing results
   - Treat step

4. **Complete**
   Reviews the service experience and client satisfaction, offers product recommendations, expresses appreciation and provides follow-up
   - Teach step

CONNECT

Ways to communicate and build your relationship with your client are:

- Meet and greet the client with a welcoming smile and a pleasant tone of voice.
- Be friendly and communicate clearly to build rapport and develop a relationship with them.
- Preview the client record for returning clients and review the client intake form for first-time clients.

CONSULT

The consultation is crucial to the facial treatment, even for returning clients. You can discuss any concerns and ensure there are no contraindications or medical issues that could pose a problem. This part of the 4 Cs includes the Observe and Analyze steps discussed in the *Skin Assessment and Recommendation System* lesson.

Every time a client visits, review records and comments from the last treatment and make sure there are no changes needed. Best practice is to have the client confirm there are no changes to their information and sign the agreement.

Ask questions to discover client needs:

- Assess the facts and think through your recommendations after reading the completed skin charting form.
- Explain your recommended solutions, products and price of the service. Think of today's service and future services.
- Gain feedback and consent from your client

Use open questions to:
- Discover client's needs
- Encourage client to talk
- Prevent clients from answering with a simple "Yes" or "No"

For example:
- "Tell me about your lifestyle/activities."
- "What is your normal facial care procedure?"
- "What other treatments have you had?"

SKIN ASSESSMENT AND RECOMMENDATION SYSTEM TREATMENT PLAN

As you learned in the *Skin Assessment and Recommendation System* lesson, there are four steps to complete within the system:

» Observe
» Analyze
» Treat
» Teach

The Consult service essential is where you perform Observe and Analyze steps. This includes:

» Review client intake form.
» Analyze client's face and complete appropriate sections of the skin charting form.
» Complete your observations in the skin charting form summary.
» Fill out the appropriate section(s) of the treatment record.

CREATE

Next you will perform the facial using the best products, tools and devices based on your client's skin analysis. This is the Treat step. Products identified here can also be included in the client's home-care program, presented in the Teach step.

During the facial treatment, use methods that ensure client comfort. Before the treatment begins, make your client aware of the steps so they can relax during the facial.

Guidelines to Ensure Client Comfort:

» Protect client by practicing infection control procedures throughout the service.
» Consider and address each client's mobility needs, such as supporting a client's knees with a bolster; be aware of the client's body language.
» Use appropriate draping for the client, depending on their needs.
» Ensure all necessary equipment is at hand to minimize noise and avoid a disjointed treatment.
» Stay focused on delivering the treatment to the best of your ability; talking during the treatment may be difficult and distracting for both of you.

Watch for Client's Body Language

Negative	Positive
» Looking away	» Eye contact
» Tense shoulders	» Relaxed body
» Clenched hands	» Open hands
» Flinching	» Gentle dozing off

Always follow appropriate infection control guidelines according to your regulatory agency.

COMPLETE

Complete includes the Teach step—explaining home-care product recommendations, instructions and a future treatment plan. Complete is as important as the analysis. Gathering feedback and answering questions at the end of the service—with your client's goals in mind—helps clarify how they can get the results they want.

As the tranquil facial experience ends, be sure to keep the tempo consistent, and avoid rushing them to get ready. Carefully remove all head protection, such as the headband and head towel, ensuring the client stays comfortable. You should also assist the client to sit up and allow time for them to get dressed.

> **To solidify your relationship with your client during the Complete phase of the facial service, follow these guidelines:**

- Request feedback from your client.
- Provide aftercare advice once the client is ready and guide them on how to take care of their skin at home.
- Discuss with them:
  - Potential concerns
  - Results of their skin analysis
  - Suitable products
  - Application of products
  - Lifestyle changes (if applicable)
  - Importance of hydration
- Escort client to retail area:
  - Recommend products to maintain appearance and condition of skin
  - Inform client that you keep these products in stock for purchase
  - Record recommended products on client treatment record and treatment plan for future visits
  - Invite your client to make a purchase
- Escort client to the reception area, encourage them to prebook for next time and ask for referrals.
- Thank client for visiting the salon/spa and leave them with a warm goodbye.
- Discard single-use items, clean and disinfect multi-use supplies.
- Change treatment table linens and prepare for the next client.

Following the treatment, remember to record:

- Details of facial within the treatment record.
- Recommended products/services for future visits.
- Any reactions to the treatment or client feedback
- Aftercare with any individual notes.
- If applicable, patch-testing results with the date and area identified.

FACIAL TREATMENT ROOM GUIDELINES

Creating a tranquil and well-organized treatment room is essential for your comfort as well as your client's, so you can work efficiently, and clients can relax and unwind.

Key areas for you to keep in mind are:

» Treatment room preparation
» Treatment room setup
» Device troubleshooting

FACIAL TREATMENT ROOM – PREPARATION

Your performance will be competent and timely with proper preparation. While you work in your treatment room, think about ideas for the best, most efficient flow for you. Having products, tools and devices placed in the correct spots—and your treatment table placed well for ergonomic needs—helps you prepare. Following are key areas for treatment room preparation.

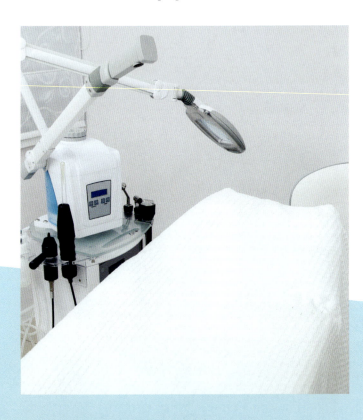

> **"I am not a product of my circumstances; by failing to prepare, you are preparing to fail."**
> —Benjamin Franklin

Lighting
» Make sure it's bright enough for you to work, but dark enough for a relaxing environment.
» Enhance lighting when working on smaller areas of the face, such as eyebrow or lip waxing, by using a magnifying lamp.

Temperature
» Balance temperature to be warm enough for the client and cool enough for you.
» Keep most products, especially clay-based products, cool for good application.
» Use recommended treatment room temperature at 70°-75°F (21°-24°C).
» Drape clients using appropriate blankets.

Ventilation
» Provide adequate ventilation to remove odors and moisture (humidity).
» Keep air moving to ensure freshness and cleanliness.
» Add essential oils to a humidifier to enhance the relaxation and luxury of the treatment room.

Ergonomics
» Position and organize the work cart or workstation in a convenient manner; products should be situated in order of use to enable a smooth and efficient service.
» Try to obtain and apply each product seamlessly without too much noise or movement for client comfort.
» Position the treatment table at a height that helps you maintain good posture; keep in mind that the client must be able to easily access the treatment table using either an adjustable table or a footstool.
» Tuck away any loose wires on equipment safely to avoid any hazard.

Hygiene
» Ensure all infection control procedures are followed for all clients.
» Have clean draping, headbands and towels ready.

FACIAL TREATMENT ROOM – SETUP

Your treatment room setup may not always be in your control, but you can choose where to place your products, tools and devices to meet your specific ergonomic needs. Try to start your workday at least 30 minutes before your first client to make sure all your supplies are available before you begin. This will prevent stress and rushing that can put your client on edge. Setting up for any treatment should be carefully planned, and all essential products, tools and equipment should be stocked and ready for use.

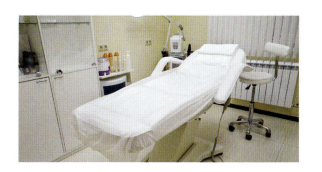

Treatment Table 	» Drape in preparation for the client, with all the necessary towels; refer to the *Facial Treatment Skills* lesson for proper draping options. » Clean facial drape set out for client. » Set table height for client to easily access.
Hot-Towel Cabinet 	» Fill cabinet with the appropriate number of towels for the treatment and be sure it's turned on.
Work Cart 	» Place paper or disposable towels on top of cart. » Have products arranged in order of use; be sure additional items used after skin analysis are easily accessible. » Ensure that all lids and dispensers are clean and work properly. » Check to see that all water bowls are clean and prepared. » Arrange brushes, tools and supplies in order of use.
Steamer 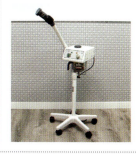	» Ensure distilled water only is added to the reservoir and ready for use. » Test steamer before placing over face to avoid spitting. » Be sure average distance from client's face is 12"-18" (30-45 cm). » Never put cold water in a warm steamer. » Follow manufacturer's instructions on how to use and clean steamer and amount of water needed. » Improper care of a steamer can result in mineral build-up on the heating element. See the *Facial Treatment Products, Tools, Supplies and Equipment* lesson for directions on maintenance.
Infection Control 	» Prepare disinfection area with proper disinfectant, containers and cleanser. » Disinfection area should be clean of debris. » Be sure that sink is cleaned with no visible debris. » Have single-use gloves readily available. » Place trash can close to work area and cover with lid.

107E.4 | FACIAL TREATMENT GUEST EXPERIENCE

FACIAL TREATMENT ROOM – DEVICE TROUBLESHOOTING

Having equipment fail right before your client arrives can be frustrating. It's important to start your day by turning on and verifying everything works before you get started.

Here are some common issues and how to handle them.

The steamer won't turn on...	» Make sure timer dial is turned on and there is enough distilled water in reservoir. » Check that an electrical fuse has not been tripped at the breaker box. » Check cords and make sure steamer is plugged into wall outlet. » Check steamer fuse (located underneath steamer case); this generally is a button or lever you can push to reset.
The steamer is spitting...	» Turn machine off. » Clean with coffee pot cleaner or white vinegar. » Re-fill and turn on. » If spitting still occurs, re-clean and call manufacturer.
Steamer ozone will not turn on...	» Turn machine off and unplug. » Reset steamer fuse. » Turn on again, let steam start then turn on ozone. » Check for light to turn on. » If the ozone light is not turning on, call the manufacturer; do not try to change this bulb yourself.
The magnifying lamp is flashing...	» Light element may be about to fail. » Turn off light and unplug. » Light bulb could need changing or fuse may need replacing.
Hot cabinet will not heat up...	» Unplug, clean, then plug in again. » If cabinet still won't heat up, call manufacturer.

FACIAL TREATMENT CARE AND SAFETY GUIDELINES

Keeping your client safe and providing exceptional care is the core of what you do every day. Causing harm due to negligence can end your career and cause lasting damage to your client. Not knowing is not a defense. The key areas to consider are:

» Contraindications

» Cautions

» Client concerns

FACIAL TREATMENT – CONTRAINDICATIONS

Contraindications refer to conditions that prevent treatment. These present in two ways:
1. Medical conditions and medications disclosed by your client
2. Visual signs, such as some primary and secondary lesions, injury or irritation

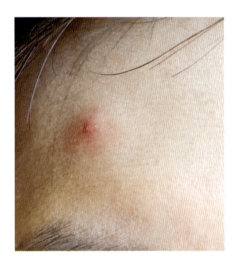
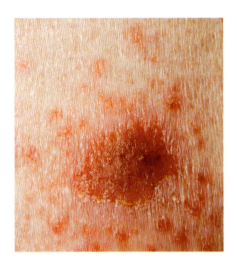

An esthetician is not allowed to diagnose medical conditions, so trying to determine a contraindication can be challenging if your client will not disclose information.

On the skin charting form, you will see an area that identifies which medical issues should prevent treatment. When contraindications such as these are presented, you must stop treatment and refer to a physician.

Here are some general guidelines and visual signs of medical conditions and medications that clients may or may not disclose. They are considered contraindications for a facial treatment. The only way to determine whether to perform a service will be based on what you see on the skin. In general, if the skin looks odd, inflamed or shows any openings, do not proceed.

Treatment is prohibited on clients with the conditions on the following chart unless otherwise noted. Refer to the lesson on *Skin Diseases and Disorders* for more specific information on this topic.

107E.4 | FACIAL TREATMENT GUEST EXPERIENCE

MEDICAL CONDITIONS/MEDICATIONS	ALERT	VISUAL SIGNS	TREATMENT DETAILS
Autoimmune Disorders » Lupus » Psoriasis	Avoid treatment	» Butterfly rash » Bumpy, red patches covered with white scales	» Avoid treatment when rash or flare-up is present » Service cannot be performed
Known Allergies » Latex gloves	Avoid treatment	» Rash » Hives » Skin redness » Itching	» Avoid treatment using known allergen
Active Infection » Virus » MRSA » Bacteria » Influenzas » HIV/AIDS » Rhinovirus (cold) » Tuberculosis » Shingles	Avoid treatment	» Rash » Swollen lymph nodes » Legions » Red, swollen, pus-filled bump » Abnormal sweating	» Active infections are a contraindication » Service cannot be performed » Use caution – HIV/AIDS is NOT a contraindication, but standard precautions should be followed
Viral Skin Infections » Herpes Simplex (active outbreak) » Herpes Zoster (shingles) » Warts » Papilloma » Tinea Corporis » Candida Albicans	Avoid treatment	» Rash » Swollen lymph nodes » Open cold sores » Small grainy skin growths with tiny black dots » White spots in mouth that resemble cottage cheese	» Active infections are a contraindication and service cannot be performed
Bacterial Skin Infections » Impetigo » Boils » Bacterial Conjunctivitis » Blepharitis » Stye » Cellulitis	Avoid treatment	» Red sores » Honey-colored crusts » Red swollen pus-filled bump » Red/pink eyes with thick mucus » Red lump on eyelid with yellow spot at middle	» Active infections are a contraindication and service cannot be performed
Skin Diseases » Eczema	Avoid treatment	» Itchy rash » Small vesicles	» Active flare-ups are a contraindication and service cannot be performed
Recent Surgery	Avoid treatment	» Sensitive skin » Scarring » Potential loss of sensation	» Any surgery can affect the client physically » Need physician approval
Accutane (Medication)	Avoid treatment	» Extremely dry skin » Itching » Rash » Cracks in corners of mouth	» Get physician approval

FACIAL TREATMENTS

MEDICAL CONDITIONS/MEDICATIONS	ALERT	VISUAL SIGNS	TREATMENT DETAILS
Vascular Disorder or Condition » Purpura » Ecchymosis	⛔ Avoid treatment	» Bruised, red-purple skin discoloration with or without patch formation » Tiny red spots	» Service cannot be performed
Sebaceous Gland Disorders » Acne Grade 3 » Acne Grade 4 (nodulocystic or cystic acne) » Acne excoriée (client creates areas of scratches and open sores)	⛔ Avoid treatment	» Reddened, inflamed skin » Large number of papules, pustules and nodules » Cysts	» Medical intervention required » High level of dermal scarring possible; infection can be spread without medical intervention
Sudoriferous Gland Disorder » Miliaria Rubra	⛔ Avoid treatment	» Small red vesicles » Itching and burning	» Service cannot be performed
Inflammation (Dermatitis) » Atopic Dermatitis » Contact Dermatitis » Seborrheic Dermatitis » Pseudofolliculitis Barbae » Pityriasis Rosea » Urticaria (Hives)	⛔ Avoid treatment	» Red plaques » Itching and possibly burning » Rough sandpaper feel » Red, swollen rash » Rash with scales » Hives » Flakiness	» Service cannot be performed
Infestations » Scabies » Pediculosis	⛔ Avoid treatment	» Intense itching » Rash which resembles tiny, red spots or insect bites » Tiny crab-like bugs or white nits on hairstrand	» Service cannot be performed
Lesions (Primary and Secondary) » Plaque » Crust » Wheal » Excoriation » Cyst » Scale » Vesicle » Fissure » Bullae » Ulcer » Nodule	⛔ Avoid treatment ⚠️ Use caution (avoid the area)	» Refer to lesson on *Skin Diseases and Disorders* for specific descriptions	» Avoid treatment or use caution depending on the type of lesion
Recent Sunburn	⛔ Avoid treatment ⚠️ Use caution (avoid the area)	» Painful reddened skin	» Avoid treatment if sunburn is on face » Use caution if sunburn is on the back or other part of the body; client won't be able to lay comfortably on the treatment table » If client is requesting a soothing treatment, be sure that the sunburn is not within the last 48 hours
Skin Cancer Growth	⛔ Avoid treatment	Signs include: » Asymmetry » Diameter » Border » Elevated » Color	» Avoid treatment on area of cancerous growth, biopsy or removal unless healed

FACIAL TREATMENT – CAUTIONS

Many medical conditions are not considered a contraindication for treatment. Instead, you can make modifications that allow you to perform the service without causing harm. Different modalities will require alternative modifications; refer to the *Facial Treatments With Devices* area of study for more information.

Here is a set of guidelines of modifications to make when dealing with potential cautions during a facial treatment.

DESCRIPTION	ALERT	DESCRIPTION/MODIFICATION
Pregnancy	Use caution	» Be aware of the client's needs and additional concerns; support and accommodate needs
Cancer	Use caution	» Important to know current state of cancer (active vs. remission) and if lymph nodes have been removed » If lymph nodes are removed, do not massage the area until further training has been received » Physician approval is required to perform services on patients actively being treated; remission doesn't require physician approval, but adjustments may be made based on client needs » Adjust device use, massage direction and pressure » It's important to seek more information when working with cancer patients; avoid products with high levels of active ingredients and modalities that are highly stimulating » LED devices are safe for clients with cancer
Diabetes	Use caution	» Can cause impaired healing, reactions are common; effects of glycation accelerated » Modalities – Chemical/mechanical exfoliation; limit mechanical exfoliation modalities; provide post-care follow-up and clear directions to avoid healing complications
Epilepsy	Use caution	» Bright light can be a trigger, confirm with client » Modalities – Light therapy, use of magnifying lamp
Heart Conditions/High Blood Pressure	Use caution	» Adjust client's position; some drugs can cause additional sensitivity; heat treatments » Modalities – Raise head when client is on treatment table, help client get off table » Heart rhythms and pacemakers can be affected by electrical treatment » Modify massage, as increased circulation could present a risk for clients with high blood pressure or a prior stroke
Thyroid Disease	Use caution	» Disorders can have direct effect on skin health; dryness, sensitivity, discoloration are common » Modalities – Chemical/mechanical exfoliation; focus on hydration and pigmentation suppression products during treatment; provide post-care follow-up and clear directions to avoid healing complications
Neck/Back Pain	Use caution	» Positioning for comfort and stability is essential » Modalities – Help client get on and off the table; use bolsters and heated table pad

DESCRIPTION	ALERT	DESCRIPTION/MODIFICATION
Hormone Issues	⚠️ Use caution	» Potential increased dryness, itchiness and sensitivity » Improvements will be limited if not addressed
Eye Disorders	⚠️ Use caution	» Eye disorders and allergies can cause extreme eye sensitivity » Modalities – Cover eyes completely with appropriate eye pads, use eye cream designed for sensitivity
Autoimmune Diseases & Disorders	⚠️ Use caution	» Flares can cause increased sensitivity » Lupus – No treatment when butterfly rash is present » Modalities – Position for comfort; help client get on and off treatment table
Chronic Pain	⚠️ Use caution	» Sensitivity to touch and light, general chronic stress » Modalities – Position for comfort; help client get on and off treatment table; use heated table pad; watch massage pressure » Metal used as bone or joint replacement is a contraindication for some esthetic devices
Known Allergies	⚠️ Use caution	» Verify with client types of triggers or ingredients that cause reactions » Modalities – Use caution with steam on asthma; check client comfort; watch breathing and place maximum distance from client
Sensitive, Redness-Prone Skin	⚠️ Use caution	» Redness could intensify; avoid heat, harsh scrubs, stimulating massage, mechanical treatment » Use caution with steam; don't apply too close to skin

Cosmetic Injections	⚠️ Use caution	» Cosmetic injections require a specific waiting period before treatment:
		  » Neuromodulators – Paralyze the muscles; 48 hours
		  » Fillers – 14 days

Hair Removal (Waxing/Electrolysis/Laser)	⚠️ Use caution	» Do not perform exfoliation within 24 hours after hair removal
Chemical Peels (1 month)	⚠️ Use caution	» Medical-level chemical peels require 1 month before services that involve exfoliation can be performed; use caution with steam and heat
Laser Treatment (1 month)	⚠️ Use caution	» Laser resurfacing requires 1 month before exfoliation is performed; gentle hydrating facial without steam and massage can help soothe » Home care for sensitive skin is essential » Hair removal – 2 weeks » Intense pulsed light therapy (IPL) – 2 weeks

Medication side effects vary based on the individual. Here are some general guidelines for modifications to implement. Be sure to rely on what you see on the skin and what the disclosed medical concerns are first.

MEDICATIONS	EFFECT ON SKIN/ MODIFICATIONS
Diabetes medications	Potential rashes and itching, treat as sensitive skin
Thyroid medications	Potential thinning skin, dryness, heat sensitivity
Anti-Depressants	Potential photosensitivity, rash, bruising
Heart/Blood Pressure medications	Photosensitivity, rash
Sleep medications	Potential "pins and needles" feeling in hands, arms and legs; rash
Pain medications	Potential allergic reaction: hives, itching, rash
Acne medications	Can cause skin to blister or peel; avoid peeling/drying agents such as alpha-hydroxy acids (AHAs), scrubs, microdermabrasion and rotating brush See *Hair Removal* area of study for waxing/hair removal restrictions.
Antibiotics	Photosensitivity, sensitive skin
Blood Thinners	May cause bleeding or bruising; require physician's permission
Corticosteroids	Can cause thinning of the skin that leads to blistering or injury; avoid any stimulating or exfoliating treatment

INDUSTRY CONNECTION

How to Deal With a Contraindication

It can be disappointing for a client when you can't do what they want. Sometimes saying "no" is the right thing to do for their safety. Suggesting alternative relaxing services can prevent you from losing a client. For example, your client has come in for a facial but has cold sores on their upper lip. How would you handle this? Here are some ideas:

1. Explain why a service could continue to harm them, e.g., "Cold sores can spread."
2. Provide an alternative service such as a body treatment.
3. Give options for re-booking and guidelines on when they can get a service again.
4. Refer to a physician if unknown or suspicious lesions are present.

Always follow appropriate infection control guidelines according to your regulatory agency.

FACIAL TREATMENT – CONCERNS

As an esthetician, you'll deal with many types of clients with specialized needs. Their response to a facial treatment will be varied, so you need to know what potential contra-actions can happen. Additional training may be necessary to help clients with specialized needs, such as cancer patients and those with diseases or disabilities.

Some basic steps can be taken during the service to keep the client safe when contra-actions occur. Additionally, there are cues as to when referral to a medical professional is required.

DISCOVER**MORE**

What Is a Contra-Action?
Contra-actions refer to situations that may arise during or after a service. Client feedback and visual indicators help you judge how the client's skin is responding. An example is an allergic reaction to face and eye products: the client may experience sensitivity, a burning sensation or redness that will not subside after an exfoliation product.

FACIAL TREATMENT GUEST EXPERIENCE

CONCERNS OR CONTRA-ACTIONS	WHAT TO DO
Tattoos or Permanent Makeup	» If inflamed or recently performed service, avoid area. » Services such as a light chemical exfoliation can be done to brighten tattoos on the body when they are healed.
Piercings	» Have client remove piercing (jewelry or piece), if possible. » Avoid area of piercing when performing massage. » Be aware of restrictions on some device use; refer to *Facial Treatments With Devices* area of study.
Erythema Inflammation	» Discontinue treatment.
Rashes » Temporary pustules and papules » Temporary swelling	» Remove products. » If necessary, use a cold compress to soothe skin.
Allergic Reaction (Face and eye products) **Sensitivity or Burning Sensation**	» Remove all products immediately and apply a cold compress. » If product entered eye, use an eye bath to flush the eye. » Record information on treatment record.
Cancer Requires additional training	» Verify stage of cancer treatment with your client. » Verify medical approval for treatment requested (this will come from the client). » Identify product ingredient sensitivities. » Provide proper support for comfort. » Identify if lymph nodes have been removed and location; modify massage when appropriate. » Limit heat treatments if skin is sensitive. » Use a positive, respectful attitude when discussing their challenges. » Do not provide feedback about the negative outcome of any cancer experience you have personally had. » Do listen compassionately; have sympathy for their situation.
Disability	» Verify type of disability and what adjustment your client needs. » Check in with your client often about their comfort. » Do not be afraid to ask detailed questions that pertain to their comfort. » Avoid pressing for answers if client does not want to discuss. » Provide proper body positioning and support with bolsters. » Utilize a treatment table that is adjustable for client to access. » Consider your disabled client's needs and be sure cabinets, dressers, lockers and beds are adjusted to appropriate heights and positions so clients can easily access them with or without assistance. » Follow all regulatory laws such as ADA (American With Disabilities Act) for your area. » Workplace needs to accommodate any equipment, such as a wheelchair, with ease.

FACIAL TREATMENT – CARE AND SAFETY CHART

The following care and safety guidelines before and during facial treatment services will help:

» Ensure your safety and that of your client
» Prevent contamination and cross-contamination
» Contribute to the salon/spa care

PERSONAL CARE	CLIENT CARE PRIOR TO THE SERVICE	CLIENT CARE DURING THE SERVICE	SALON/SPA CARE
Check that your personal standards of hygiene minimize the spread of infection.	Have client put on gown. Have client remove jewelry and piercings. Drape client using the appropriate draping: cocoon wrap or layered method.	Use eye pads to protect and soothe the eyes when analyzing the skin or applying masks.	Follow health and safety guidelines, including cleaning and disinfecting procedures.
Wash hands and dry thoroughly with a single-use towel.	Use clean linens with each client.	Be aware of skin sensitivity or cautions.	Ensure equipment, including the treatment table, sink, table and counter areas are clean and disinfected before and after every service.
Disinfect workstation.	Identify contraindications and cautions for treatment such as: » Medical conditions » Medications » Disabilities	Work carefully around nonremovable jewelry/piercings.	Promote a professional image by assuring your workstation is clean and organized throughout the service.
Clean and disinfect tools appropriately.	Keep lids clean and tightly closed on product jars to avoid spillage and contamination.	Be aware of nonverbal cues the client may be conveying.	Keep tools dry to avoid a short circuit when using electrical equipment.
Wear single-use gloves and other personal protective equipment, as required.	Review client intake form. Complete skin charting form, treatment record and treatment plan.	Remove all products from jars with a clean spatula.	Keep labels on all containers and store products in a cool place to protect shelf-life.
Refer to your area's regulatory agency guidelines for proper mixing/handling of disinfectant solution.		If any tools or multi-use supplies are dropped, be sure to pick them up, then clean and disinfect.	Clean/mop water spillage from floor to avoid accidental falls.
Follow ergonomic guidelines for personal safety (see *Ergonomics* lesson).		Store soiled towels in dry, covered receptacle until laundered.	

FACIAL TREATMENT SERVICE CLIENT GUIDELINES

To ensure your client's comfort and satisfaction during the facial treatment service, combine the facial treatment steps with effective guidelines to produce predictable results.

PRE-CLEANSE	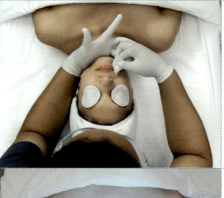	» Use caution when removing eye makeup; do not oversaturate cotton pads to avoid getting product into eyes. » Use fast, stimulating cleansing movements.
ANALYZE	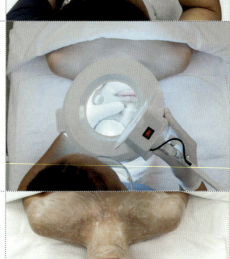	» Be sure magnifying lamp arm is fully secured to avoid it falling on your client. » Make sure that client's eyes are completely covered. » Wear gloves when analyzing the face.
CLEANSE AND TONE		» Use the appropriate cleanser based on skin analysis. » Apply product with long, sweeping strokes. » Use cleansing application movements at a slower rhythm for deep cleansing. » Remove cleanser using warm towels. » Apply toner to the skin using cotton pad. » Blot excess moisture with a tissue.
EXFOLIATE		» Check for sensitivity before using a granular scrub. » Use fast circular movements; slight erythema or redness is acceptable. » Check your client's comfort while using the scrub.

TREAT		» Serums, ampoules and other active treatments can cause tingling, and this is normal, so let your client know about the potential. » Apply steam and desincrustation gel before performing extractions. » Do not use deep pressure to remove comedones.
MASSAGE		» Be sure to check in with the client about how your touch feels and that the pressure is not too deep.
MASK		» Setting masks can make claustrophobia worse; check with your client before using.
PROTECT		» Use serums, eye cream and moisturizers that are recommended for your client's home-care routine. » Avoid SPF if service is being performed in the evening.

DISCOVER**MORE**

How Do You Feel?

Poet Maya Angelou is quoted as saying, "I've learned that people will forget what you said, people will forget what you did, but people will never forget how you made them feel." Being sensitive to how people feel will determine your success in any relationship, whether it be romantic, friendship or professional.

People will remember how safe and secure they felt with the cocoon wrap during the facial. They'll also remember the relaxing and soothing feeling that occurred because you were consistent with the massage movements and didn't break contact during the facial massage. Incorporating the four Service Essentials throughout the service will ensure your guest feels welcome and taken care of in a warm, professional manner. There are many ways you can impact how people feel. What will be your signature actions that help people remember your facial treatment?

Always follow appropriate infection control guidelines according to your regulatory agency.

FACIAL TREATMENT OVERVIEWS AND RUBRICS

The Facial Treatment Overview identifies the three areas of all facial treatments:

1. Preparation	Preparation provides a brief overview of the steps to follow before you begin a facial treatment.
2. Procedure	Procedure provides an overview of the steps that you will use during a facial treatment to ensure predictable results.
3. Completion	Completion provides an overview of the steps to follow after performing a facial treatment to ensure guest satisfaction.

A performance (assessment) rubric is a document that identifies defined criteria where levels of performance can be measured objectively. After each overview is an example of a rubric that your instructor might choose to use for scoring. The rubrics are divided into three main areas—Preparation, Procedure and Completion. Each area is further divided into step-by-step procedures that will ensure client safety and satisfaction.

FACIAL TREATMENT OVERVIEW

FACIAL TREATMENT PREPARATION	» Wash hands; and set up cleansed and disinfected workstation. » Arrange disinfected tools, supplies, products; plug in devices and test; dispense gloves. » Set up treatment table; drape table; place gown on table; place wet towels in hot cabinet. » Perform Observe step in Skin Assessment and Recommendation system.

FACIAL TREATMENT PROCEDURE	» Drape and cover client appropriately.
	» Apply hand sanitizer and gloves.
	» Pre-Cleanse
	   » Remove makeup.
	   » Perform superficial cleanse.
	» Analyze
	   » Identify Fitzpatrick skin type and skin conditions using magnifying and Wood's lamp.
	   » Complete summary analysis.
	» Cleanse and Tone
	   » Apply cleanser evenly over upper chest, neck and face.
	   » Perform cleansing application movements.
	   » Remove cleanser using warm towels or wet gauze.
	   » Apply toner to upper chest, neck and face.
	   » For acne facial - Perform another cleanse using appropriate application and removal procedure.
	» Exfoliate
	   » Turn on steamer.
	   » Apply exfoliant using appropriate procedure; apply steam to skin.
	   » Remove exfoliant with warm steam towel.
	   » For acne facial - A granular exfoliation is not performed.
	» Treat
	   » Perform extractions on comedones using appropriate procedure.
	   » Apply treatment serum using application movements.
	   » For acne facial - Perform extractions using appropriate products and tools.
	» Massage
	   » Apply massage medium using application movements.
	   » Perform massage movements.
	   » Remove massage medium using steamed towel or wet gauze.
	   » Apply toner to upper chest, neck and face.
	   » For acne facial- No massage is performed.
	» Mask
	   » Apply mask using application movements and let sit according to manufacturer's instructions.
	   » Remove mask using towels or wet gauze then tone.
	» Protect
	   » Apply eye cream.
	   » Apply serum, moisturizer, and sun protection over upper chest, neck and face.

FACIAL TREATMENT COMPLETION	» Reinforce client's satisfaction with overall salon/spa experience. » Make professional product recommendations. » Prebook client's next appointment. » End guest's visit with warm and personal goodbye. » Discard single-use supplies, disinfect tools and multi-use supplies, disinfect workstation and arrange in proper order. » Place used towels in a closed container or place in washing machine. » Change treatment table linens to prepare for next client. » Wash hands. » Complete client record.

FACIAL TREATMENT RUBRIC

Allotted Time: 60 Minutes

Student Name: _____ ID Number: _____

Instructor: _____ Date: _____ Start Time: _____ End Time: _____

FACIAL TREATMENT (Live Model) – Each scoring item is marked with either a "Yes" or "No". Each "Yes" counts for one point. Total number of points attainable is 33.

CRITERIA	YES	NO	INSTRUCTOR ASSESSMENT
PREPARATION: *Did student...*			
1. Wash their hands?	☐	☐	
2. Set up workstation with properly labeled supplies?	☐	☐	
3. Place disinfected tools and supplies at a visibly clean workstation?	☐	☐	
4. Properly drape treatment table?	☐	☐	
5. Apply appropriate PPE?	☐	☐	
Connect: *Did student...*			
6. Meet and greet client with a welcoming smile and pleasant tone of voice?	☐	☐	
7. Communicate to build rapport and develop a relationship with client?	☐	☐	
Consult: *Did student...*			
8. Ask questions to discover client's wants and needs?	☐	☐	
9. Gain feedback and consent from client before proceeding?	☐	☐	
PROCEDURE: *Did student...*			
10. Properly drape client and prepare for service?	☐	☐	
11. Apply hand sanitizer and gloves if required?	☐	☐	
Create: *Did student...*			
12. Perform pre-cleanse step using appropriate makeup remover procedure?	☐	☐	
13. Perform pre-cleanse step using appropriate superficial cleanse procedure?	☐	☐	
14. Analyze client's skin using appropriate procedures and record any possible contraindications to service?	☐	☐	
15. Cleanse client's skin thoroughly using the appropriate products and application and removal procedures? For acne facial performed second cleanse?	☐	☐	
16. Apply toner to skin using the appropriate products and procedures?	☐	☐	
17. Apply appropriate exfoliant product using the proper application and removal procedures?	☐	☐	
18. Treat the skin using the appropriate products and procedures based on the client's skin analysis?	☐	☐	
19. Obtain and apply massage cream using appropriate application procedure? Note that massage can be omitted for acne facial.	☐	☐	
20. Perform massage movements over the upper chest, neck and face with accuracy; thoroughly remove product?	☐	☐	
21. Apply mask using appropriate product and application procedure?	☐	☐	
22. Remove mask using appropriate removal techniques?	☐	☐	
23. Apply toner to skin using the appropriate products and procedures?	☐	☐	
24. Apply the appropriate products and procedures to moisturize and protect the skin?	☐	☐	
COMPLETION *(Complete):* *Did student...*			
25. Ask questions and look for verbal and nonverbal cues to determine client's level of satisfaction?	☐	☐	
26. Make professional product recommendations?	☐	☐	
27. Ask client to make a future appointment?	☐	☐	
28. End guest's visit with a warm and personal goodbye?	☐	☐	
29. Discard single-use supplies?	☐	☐	
30. Disinfect tools, multi-use supplies and equipment and arrange in proper order?	☐	☐	
31. Complete service within scheduled time?	☐	☐	
32. Complete client record?	☐	☐	
33. Wash their hands following the service?	☐	☐	

Comments: _____

TOTAL POINTS = _____ ÷ 33 = _____ %

CLIENT INTAKE FORM

Last Name: _____ First Name: _____ Date: __/__/____

Email: _____ Phone: (____) ____-____ Birthday: __/__/____

Address: _____

City/State: _____ Zip: _____ Occupation: _____

Climate: _____ Sex: ☐ Female ☐ Male

How did you hear about us? _____ Referral: _____

What skin improvements would you like to see? _____

Women: Are you pregnant or lactating? ☐ Yes ☐ No   Men: Do you experience irritation from shaving? ☐ Yes ☐ No

HEALTH HISTORY

Cancer (skin or other)	☐ Yes ☐ No	Infection (virus, bacteria)		☐ Yes ☐ No
Diabetes	☐ Yes ☐ No	HIV/AIDS		☐ Yes ☐ No
Autoimmune Disease (Lupus, RA, MS etc.)	☐ Yes ☐ No	Eye Disorders		☐ Yes ☐ No
Thyroid Disease	☐ Yes ☐ No	Chronic Pain (fibromyalgia, migraine etc.)		☐ Yes ☐ No
Neck/Back Pain	☐ Yes ☐ No	Epilepsy		☐ Yes ☐ No
Heart Problems/Blood Pressure	☐ Yes ☐ No	Hormone Issues (PCOS, Endometriosis, menopause)		☐ Yes ☐ No
Allergies (please list)	☐ Yes ☐ No	_____		

Explanation/further details: _____

SKIN HISTORY

Recent surgery (general) the last 6 months?	☐ Yes ☐ No	Laser treatments/IPL within the last month?	☐ Yes ☐ No
Recent surgery (cosmetic) the last 6 months?	☐ Yes ☐ No	Chemical peels within the last month?	☐ Yes ☐ No
Recent cosmetic injections (Botox, filler etc.)?	☐ Yes ☐ No	Loss of skin sensation?	☐ Yes ☐ No
Recent hair removal? (waxing, laser electrolysis)	☐ Yes ☐ No	Recent sunburn?	☐ Yes ☐ No
Are you under a doctor's care for skin issues?	☐ Yes ☐ No		

DAILY MEDICATIONS

☐ Accutane   ☐ Retin-A   ☐ Diabetes   ☐ Thyroid
☐ Antibiotic   ☐ Anti-Depressant   ☐ Heart/Blood Pressure ☐ Corticosteroid
☐ Sleep/Anxiety ☐ Pain/NSAIDs   ☐ Blood Thinner   ☐ Anti-Androgen
☐ Hormones   ☐ Skin Disease   ☐ Other: _____

DAILY SKIN CARE (1x, 2x, weekly, varies)

☐ Cleanser/Toner Frequency _____   ☐ Moisturizer   Frequency _____
☐ Exfoliant/Scrub Frequency _____   ☐ SPF   Frequency _____
☐ Serum/Oil   Frequency _____   ☐ Night Cream   Frequency _____
☐ Mask   Frequency _____   ☐ Prescription Frequency _____
☐ Eye Cream   Frequency _____   ☐ Neck Cream   Frequency _____

Reasons for use (i.e. improves wrinkles etc.): _____

CLIENT INTAKE FORM (Cont'd)
LIFESTYLE

Question	Yes/No	Follow-up
Do you sleep from 6-8 hours a night?	☐ Yes ☐ No	If no, how many hours? _____
Do you smoke?	☐ Yes ☐ No	Cigarettes or other: _____
Do you have chronic stress?	☐ Yes ☐ No	What is your level? ☐ Low ☐ Medium ☐ High
Do you exercise regularly?	☐ Yes ☐ No	☐ Cardio ☐ Weights ☐ Yoga ☐ Other: _____
Do you use hormone replacement therapy?	☐ Yes ☐ No	
Do you get daily UV exposure?	☐ Yes ☐ No	☐ 8+ hours ☐ Less than 5 hours ☐ Less than 1 hour
Do you drink more than 7 drinks a week of alcohol?	☐ Yes ☐ No	
Do you eat at least 3 servings of vegetables a day?	☐ Yes ☐ No	
Is your intake of sugar more than 100 cals a day?	☐ Yes ☐ No	(Examples: soda, desserts, other processed foods)
Do you drink more than 2 cups a day of caffeine?	☐ Yes ☐ No	
Do you drink 8-10 glasses of water a day?	☐ Yes ☐ No	
Do you take probiotics daily?	☐ Yes ☐ No	
Do you take vitamin D3 daily?	☐ Yes ☐ No	
Do you take a multivitamin daily or omega oils?	☐ Yes ☐ No	

Future Appointments/Contact:

May I call you at your phone number to confirm future appointments?	☐ Yes ☐ No
May I text you to confirm?	☐ Yes ☐ No
May I contact you via mail/email about future promotions and news?	☐ Yes ☐ No

Service Consent:

I understand, have read and completed this questionnaire truthfully. I agree that this constitutes full disclosure, and that it supersedes any previous verbal or written disclosures. I understand that withholding information or providing misinformation may result in contraindications and/or irritation to the skin from treatments received. I understand the appointment cancellation policy. The treatments I receive here are voluntary, and I release this institution and/or skin care professional from liability and assume full responsibility thereof.

Client Signature: _____ Date: _____

SKIN CHARTING FORM

Last Name: _____ First Name: _____ Date: ___/___/_____

Client age range: ☐ 16-24 ☐ 25-40 ☐ 41-50 ☐ 51-60 ☐ 61-70+   Male: Shaving irritation? ☐ | Female: Pregnant/Lactating? ☐

Reviewed client health history form? ☐ Yes ☐ No   Client daily skin care regimen verified? ☐ Yes ☐ No

Client skin history verified? ☐ Yes ☐ No   Client lifestyle factors verified? ☐ Yes ☐ No

CLIENT SKIN CARE CONCERNS (Check all that apply)

☐ Breakouts   ☐ Blackheads   ☐ Milia   ☐ Dark Circles
☐ Redness   ☐ Pigmentation   ☐ Sagging Skin   ☐ Wrinkles
☐ Rough Texture ☐ Dryness   ☐ Dehydration   ☐ Irritation
☐ Uneven Color   ☐ Other: _____

CONTRAINDICATIONS
HEALTH

Active Cancer (in treatment) ☐ Yes ☐ No   Active Infection ☐ Yes ☐ No   Diabetes ☐ Yes ☐ No

Ingredient Allergies ☐ Yes ☐ No List: _____   Latex Allergy ☐ Yes ☐ No

☐ Other: _____

MEDICATIONS

Accutane ☐ Yes ☐ No   Skin Disease ☐ Yes ☐ No

☐ Other: _____

SKIN HISTORY

Open Lesions ☐ Yes ☐ No   Sunburn ☐ Yes ☐ No   Recent Surgery ☐ Yes ☐ No

CAUTIONS/HEALTH HISTORY FACTORS

List cautions: _____

List health history factors: _____

ANALYSIS – SKIN TYPE

Location	Description	Results	Fitzpatrick Skin Type (UV Response)	
Zones _____ _____	☐ **Pore Size:** Small pore size ☐ **Skin Thickness:** Thick skin with good elasticity, usually young clients ☐ **Wood's lamp:** Shows even blue/purple fluorescence throughout face	**Normal** Balanced oil production	☐ Type 1 (I)	Highly sensitive, always burns, never tans.
			☐ Type 2 (II)	Very sun sensitive, burns easily, tans minimally.
Zones _____ _____	☐ **Pore Size:** Small pore size ☐ **Skin Thickness:** Possible thin skin ☐ **Wood's lamp:** Shows small orange dots on nose and chin	**Dry** Limited oil production	☐ Type 3 (III)	Sun sensitive, sometimes burns, slowly tans to light brown.
Zones _____ _____	☐ **Pore Size:** Mix of medium/large pores through forehead, nose ☐ **Skin Thickness:** Thick on cheeks, thin around eyes, forehead ☐ **Wood's lamp:** Shows small orange dots through t-zone	**Combination** Uneven oil production	☐ Type 4 (IV)	Minimally sun sensitive, burns minimally, always tans to moderate brown.
			☐ Type 5 (V)	Sun insensitive, rarely burns, tans well.
Zones _____ _____	☐ **Pore Size:** Medium to large pores throughout face ☐ **Skin Thickness:** Generally thick ☐ **Wood's lamp:** Shows small orange dots throughout face and hairline, always feel oil in skin	**Oily** Widespread oil production	☐ Type 6 (VI)	Sun insensitive, rarely burns, tans well.

SKIN CHARTING FORM (Cont'd)

Last Name: _____ First Name: _____ Date: ___/___/_____

ANALYSIS (LOOK/TOUCH/ASK)

Location	Look		Touch/Ask	Results
Zones: _____ _____	Color: ☐ Inflammation/ Redness (erythema) ☐ Flushed appearance (microcirculation)	Structure: ☐ Broken capillaries (telangiectasia) ☐ Edema (swelling)	☐ Do you get irritated when touched or certain products are used? ☐ Have you been diagnosed with rosacea?	Sensitivity: ☐ Rosacea ☐ Sensitive skin ☐ Allergies
Zones: _____ _____	Color: ☐ Dull appearance (gray/yellow)	Structure: ☐ Flakiness, Roughness ☐ Comedones, Milia ☐ Pustules, Papules	☐ Use dehydration test ☐ Congestion felt below skin, rough texture ☐ Does it feel like your moisturizer never penetrates? ☐ How often are you breaking out?	Texture: ☐ Acne grades 1-2 ☐ Congested skin ☐ Dehydration
Zones: _____ _____	Color: ☐ Dull appearance ☐ Discoloration ☐ Increased redness	Structure: ☐ Loose skin (elastosis) ☐ Wrinkles (superficial to deep) ☐ Folds of skin at ears ☐ Slack muscles	☐ Use elasticity test ☐ Do you feel loose skin along your jawline?	Aging: ☐ Wrinkles (fine to deep) ☐ Sagging skin ☐ Slack muscles ☐ Dull appearance ☐ Broken Capillaries
Zones: _____ _____	Color: ☐ Discolored areas on skin ☐ Loss of color in areas, ☐ Post inflammatory pigmentation (red/brown spots)	Structure: ☐ Raised rough areas	☐ Feel pigmented areas for raised lesions ☐ Have you been diagnosed with melasma? ☐ How long after receiving an injury to your skin does the discoloration last	Pigmentation: ☐ Hyperpigmentation ☐ Melasma ☐ Hypopigmentation ☐ UV Damage
Zones: _____ _____	Color: ☐ Redness in areas of breakout (red/brown spots)	Structure: ☐ Comedones, Milia, Pustules, Papules	☐ Raised bumps on skin ☐ Congestion felt below skin ☐ How often are you breaking out? ☐ Have you been diagnosed with acne?	Acne: ☐ Acne grades 1-2 ☐ Congested skin

SUMMARY ANALYSIS (Note pore size and location on face chart)

SKIN TYPE:
☐ Normal ☐ Oily ☐ Combination ☐ Dry

Fitzpatrick Skin Type:
☐ 1 (I) ☐ 2 (II) ☐ 3 (III) ☐ 4 (IV) ☐ 5 (V) ☐ 6 (VI)

Fitzpatrick Type Caution: _____

SKIN CONDITION: Note 2 categories and location on face chart

Sensitivity	Texture	Aging	Pigmentation
☐ Rosacea ☐ Sensitive skin ☐ Allergies	☐ Acne grades 1-2 ☐ Congested skin ☐ Dehydration	☐ Wrinkles (fine to deep) ☐ Sagging skin ☐ Slack muscles ☐ Dull appearance ☐ Broken Capillaries	☐ Hyperpigmentation ☐ Melasma ☐ Hypopigmentation ☐ UV Damage

LIFESTYLE/HEALTH FACTORS:

Contraindications: _____
Cautions: _____
Diet: ☐ Caffeine ☐ Processed Food ☐ Sugar ☐ Supplements
Sleep: _____ Hours _____ ☐ Less than 6 hours
Stress level: ☐ Low ☐ Medium ☐ High
Climate: ☐ Hot Humid ☐ Mild Humid ☐ Cold Humid ☐ Dry ☐ Cold Dry
Exercise: ☐ Cardio ☐ Weights ☐ Yoga ☐ Other: _____
☐ 8+ hours ☐ 4-7 hours ☐ Less than 4 hours
Smoking/Alcohol: ☐ Smoking ☐ Alcohol: More than 7 drinks a week

Notes: _____

TREATMENT RECORD

Esthetician initials: _____

Last Name: _____ First Name: _____ Date: ___ / ___ / _____

TREATMENTS

Treatment Chosen: _____ Modifications: _____

Expected Results: _____

Skin Changes: _____

Follow-up Date: ___ / ___ / _____

Feedback: _____

SERVICE GOALS: Choose up to 2, indicate treatment focus as it relates to INCREASE, BALANCE or DECREASE Phases

☐ Sensitivity: _____

☐ Texture: _____

☐ Aging: _____

☐ Pigmentation TR: _____

☐ Acne: _____

☐ Other: _____

PRODUCTS: Select type then list product(s)

☐ Cleansers: _____ ☐ Massage Medium: _____

☐ Toner: _____ ☐ Masks: _____

☐ Treatments/Serums: _____ ☐ Moisturizers: _____

☐ Exfoliator: _____ ☐ Other: _____

SKIN WARMING

☐ Steamer ☐ Hot Towels ☐ Occlusion ☐ Device

☐ Other: _____

MASSAGE

☐ Effleurage ☐ Petrissage ☐ Tapotement ☐ Friction/Vibration

DEVICES

☐ Galvanic Current ☐ High Frequency ☐ Microdermabrasion ☐ LED

EXTRACTION

☐ Finger Technique ☐ Comedone Extractor ☐ Cotton swabs ☐ Lancets (if allowed)

NOTES

_____

_____

_____

_____

_____

TREATMENT PLAN

Last Name: _____ First Name: _____ Date: ___ / ___ / _____

RECOMMENDED TREATMENTS (3-month Plan)

TREATMENT	GOAL	COSTS	FREQUENCY / NEXT APPT
_____	_____	_____	_____
_____	_____	_____	_____
_____	_____	_____	_____
_____	_____	_____	_____
_____	_____	_____	_____
_____	_____	_____	_____

RECOMMENDED HOME CARE

AM	RECOMMENDED	CURRENT USE	PM	RECOMMENDED	CURRENT USE
Cleanse:	_____	_____	Cleanse:	_____	_____
Tone:	_____	_____	Tone:	_____	_____
Treat:	_____	_____	Treat:	_____	_____
Moisture:	_____	_____	Moisture:	_____	_____
Eye Cream:	_____	_____	Eye Cream:	_____	_____
Lip Treatment:	_____	_____	Lip Treatment:	_____	_____
SPF:	_____	_____	Neck Cream:	_____	_____

Weekly Treatment

	RECOMMENDED	CURRENT USE
Exfoliation:	_____	_____
Mask:	_____	_____

INSTRUCTIONS:

_____

_____

_____

_____

107E.4 | FACIAL TREATMENT GUEST EXPERIENCE

Always follow appropriate infection control guidelines according to your regulatory agency.

When you provide clients with an exceptional experience during facial treatments, it's an opportunity to gain loyal return business.

LESSONS LEARNED

- The service essentials related to a facial treatment are:
  - Connect: Establish rapport and builds credibility with each client
  - Consult: Analyze client needs, complete skin evaluation and obtain client consent
  - Create: Ensure client safety and comfort; stay focused to deliver the best service; explain the products to your client; teach the client at-home care maintenance
  - Complete: Request feedback; recommend products; suggest future appointment times; complete client record
- Facial treatment room guidelines include:
  - Facial treatment room preparation
  - Setup and device troubleshooting
- Care and safety guidelines for facial treatments
  - Ensure your client's comfort and satisfaction
  - Ensure your safety and that of your client
  - Prevent contamination and cross-contamination
  - Contribute to the salon/spa care

- Some facial treatment service guidelines that ensure client comfort and satisfaction when performing this service include:
  - Use gloves when touching client's face during analysis
  - Check client comfort and sensitivity before and during exfoliation
  - Check client comfort and pressure used during massage
- The three areas of a facial treatment service are:
  - Preparation – Provides a brief overview of the steps to follow before you begin a facial treatment service.
  - Procedure – Provides an overview of the steps that you will follow during a facial treatment service to ensure predictable results.
  - Completion – Provides an overview of the steps to follow after performing a facial treatment service to ensure guest satisfaction.

DRAPING, TOWEL AND TABLE PREPARATION FOR FACIAL TREATMENT
SKILLS WORKSHOP

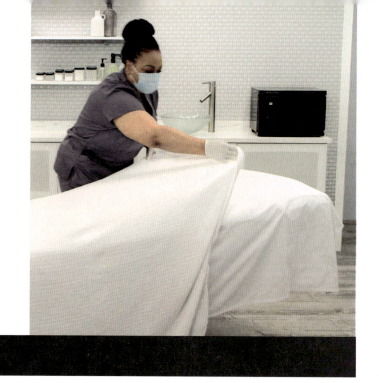

EXPLORE
How does it make you feel when a service provider hasn't properly prepared for the service you are about to receive?

INSPIRE
Draping, preparing towels and setting up the treatment table appropriately allows you to begin every facial treatment safely and professionally.

ACHIEVE
Following this *Draping, Towel and Table Preparation for Facial Treatment Skills Workshop*, you'll be able to:

» Demonstrate the proper skills to drape a client, prepare towels and prepare the table for a facial treatment

PRODUCTS, TOOLS AND SUPPLIES:

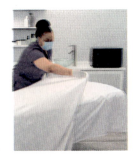

PERFORMANCE GUIDE

DRAPING, TOWEL AND TABLE PREPARATION FOR FACIAL TREATMENT SKILLS

View the video, then practice the Draping, Towel and Table Preparation for Facial Treatment procedure. Complete the self-check as you progress.

10 minutes
Commercially Accepted Time

PREPARATION

Wash and dry your hands:
- Apply hand sanitizer
- Apply gloves

Gather tools and supplies necessary to properly drape a client, prepare towels and prepare the table.

PREPARE TOWELS

1. **Disinfect sink, as applicable, prior to beginning:**
   - Follow manufacturer's instructions for disinfectant timing
   - Turn hot-towel cabinet on, following manufacturer's instructions

   Note: A large bowl filled with warm or hot water may also be used after disinfecting.

2. **Fill sink or bowl:**
   - Fill sink halfway with warm/hot water
   - If aromatherapy ingredients are used, add to water following manufacturer's instructions

3. Fold a clean cotton towel in half, widthwise.

4. Fold towel in half again.

5. Roll towel tightly, keeping ends of towel inside roll.

   Note: Many salon/spas roll the towel prior to storage in an appropriate, closed cabinet.

6. Thoroughly saturate towel by submerging in water:
   » Wring out excess water
   » Multiple towels can be prepared and submerged at once

7. Place the towel into the hot-towel cabinet:
   » Prepare and store multiple towels for use during service

COCOON WRAP

8. **Wash and dry your hands:**
   - Apply gloves
   - Apply hand sanitizer to gloves if already worn

9. **Place and turn on heated table pad:**
   - Cover pad and table with twin-size fitted sheet (table cover may also be used)

10. Drape queen-size blanket horizontally over treatment table.

11. Position queen-size cotton sheet over blanket.

12. Lay hand towel across top of table.

13. **Place one folded hand towel at top of the bed to wrap client's head:**
    - Fold this towel diagonally with ends pointed toward top of table
    - Place headband on top of towel

14. **Provide a gown for the client; ask client to put gown on:**
    - Step out of the room while client changes

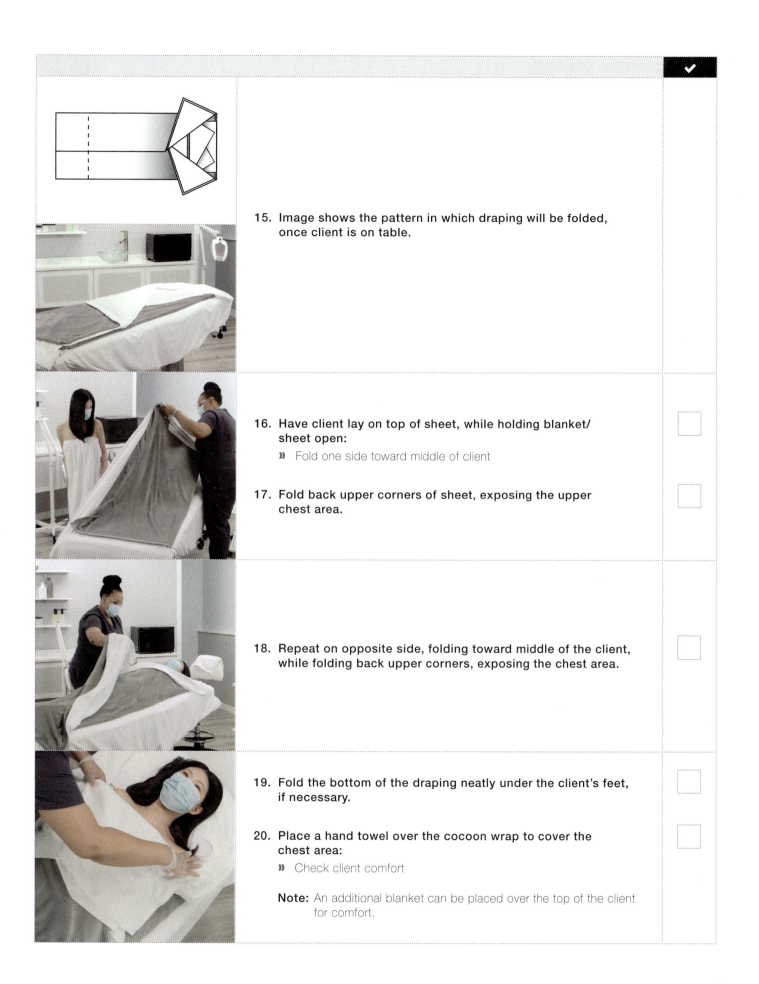

15. Image shows the pattern in which draping will be folded, once client is on table.

16. Have client lay on top of sheet, while holding blanket/sheet open:
    » Fold one side toward middle of client

17. Fold back upper corners of sheet, exposing the upper chest area.

18. Repeat on opposite side, folding toward middle of the client, while folding back upper corners, exposing the chest area.

19. Fold the bottom of the draping neatly under the client's feet, if necessary.

20. Place a hand towel over the cocoon wrap to cover the chest area:
    » Check client comfort

    Note: An additional blanket can be placed over the top of the client for comfort.

LAYERED TREATMENT-TABLE SETUP

21. **Place a heated pad on the table and turn it on:**
    - Cover pad and table with a table cover or twin-size fitted sheet
    - Lay hand towel across top of table

    Note: If using a table cover, be sure to place the fitted twin-size sheet over the top.

22. **Place one folded hand towel at top of bed to wrap client's head:**
    - Fold towel diagonally with ends pointed toward top of table
    - Place headband on top of towel

23. **Lay a twin-size sheet over the top of the entire table.**

24. **Position a twin-size duvet, blanket or comforter over the top of the sheet:**
    - Fold top of sheet down over duvet, blanket or comforter
    - Provide a gown for client; ask client to put gown on
    - Step out of the room while client changes

25. **Have client lay on top of sheet:**
    - Open sheet and blanket
    - Have client lay on top of sheet; assist client if necessary

26. **Cover client to chest:**
    - Ensure that client's skin only comes in contact with the sheet, not the blanket
    - Make sure sheet and blanket are balanced over client's body

27. **Make necessary adjustments:**
    - Add bolsters, towels, adjust temperature of bed, add/remove blankets

    Note: Application of head wrap and towel is the same as with a cocoon wrap: client's PPE can be removed at ths point.

FACIAL TREATMENTS

HEADBAND

28. **Cover client's hair (headband):**
    - Pull client's hair away from face
    - Bring one end of headband up from base of skull, around to client's forehead; hold end of headband in place and bring other end up and around to secure
    - Pull ears out from headband
    - Tuck hair in as necessary and check client comfort

    Note: Client's PPE has been removed at this point and placed in a plastic bag.

29. **Cover client's hair with towel:**
    - Tuck ends of towel to secure
    - Check client's comfort

COMPLETION

- You are now ready to move on to the pre-cleanse step of the facial.

10 minutes Commercially Accepted Time

My Speed

INSTRUCTIONS:
Record your time in comparison with the commercially accepted time. Then list here how you could improve your performance.

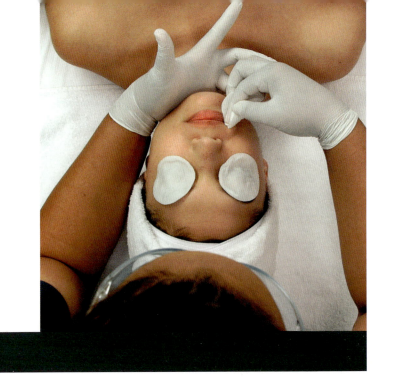

PRE-CLEANSE
SKILLS WORKSHOP

EXPLORE
Have you ever tried to examine a framed photograph closely, only to realize that dust or dirt on the glass makes it impossible?

INSPIRE
Performing a thorough pre-cleanse promotes more accurate skin analysis and sets the stage for a successful facial treatment.

ACHIEVE
Following this *Pre-Cleanse Skills Workshop*, you'll be able to:
» Demonstrate the proper skills to perform a facial pre-cleanse

PRODUCTS, TOOLS AND SUPPLIES:

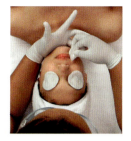

PERFORMANCE GUIDE
PRE-CLEANSE SKILLS
View the video, then practice the Pre-Cleanse procedure.
Complete the self-check as you progress.

2 minutes
Commercially Accepted Time

PREPARATION

Wash and dry your hands:
- Apply hand sanitizer
- Apply gloves

Note: Esthetician wears appropriate PPE at all times. Follow *all* applicable guidelines from regulating agencies regarding health, safety, infection control and personal protective equipment to be worn.

Set up workstation, supplies, products and treatment table:
- Include appropriate number of 4" x 4" gauze pads and cotton rounds

Note: A bowl filled with warm water should be set up on the workstation.

Prior to pre-cleanse:
- Client has been assisted onto table
- Client has been appropriately draped

REMOVE MAKEUP

1. Apply hand sanitizer to gloves if gloves are already applied.

2. Place cotton pads saturated with makeup remover on each eye:
   - Use light circular movements to help dissolve eye makeup

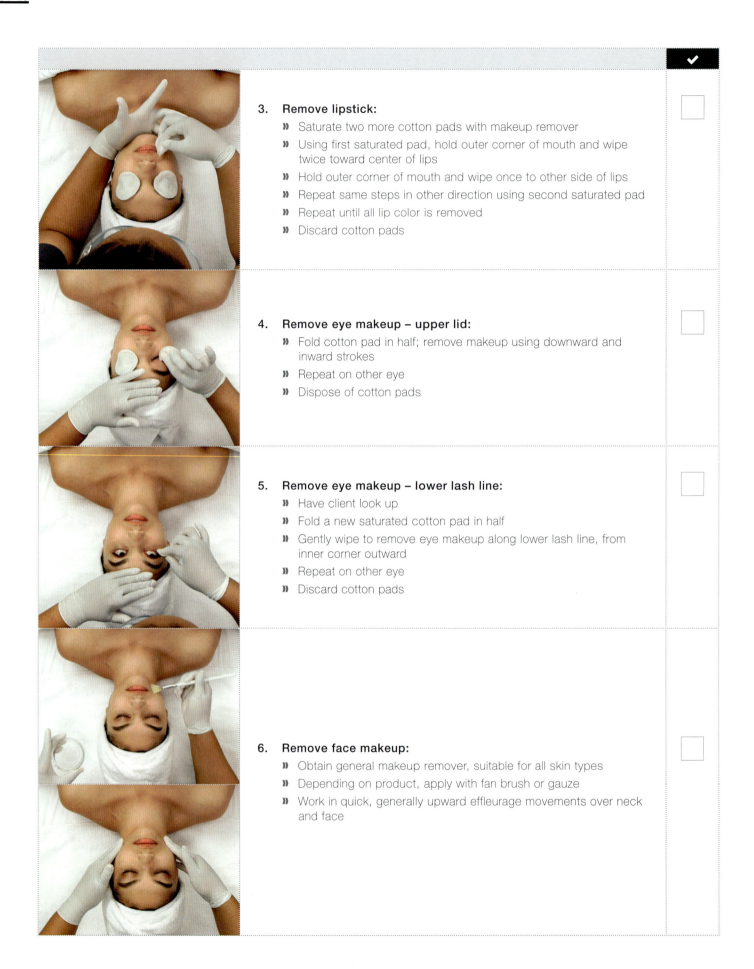

3. **Remove lipstick:**
   - Saturate two more cotton pads with makeup remover
   - Using first saturated pad, hold outer corner of mouth and wipe twice toward center of lips
   - Hold outer corner of mouth and wipe once to other side of lips
   - Repeat same steps in other direction using second saturated pad
   - Repeat until all lip color is removed
   - Discard cotton pads

4. **Remove eye makeup – upper lid:**
   - Fold cotton pad in half; remove makeup using downward and inward strokes
   - Repeat on other eye
   - Dispose of cotton pads

5. **Remove eye makeup – lower lash line:**
   - Have client look up
   - Fold a new saturated cotton pad in half
   - Gently wipe to remove eye makeup along lower lash line, from inner corner outward
   - Repeat on other eye
   - Discard cotton pads

6. **Remove face makeup:**
   - Obtain general makeup remover, suitable for all skin types
   - Depending on product, apply with fan brush or gauze
   - Work in quick, generally upward effleurage movements over neck and face

7. Remove with warm, wet gauze.

PERFORM SUPERFICIAL CLEANSE (FIRST CLEANSE)

8. Perform superficial cleanse:
   » Obtain cleanser suitable for all skin types (or for specific skin type if known)
   » Warm the product in your hands

9. Apply cleanser evenly over upper chest, neck and face:
   » Upward effleurage movements

10. Use cleansing application movements with light pressure and fast rhythm:
    » Effleurage movements (circular)
    » Work from upper chest through neck, across jawline, up to cheeks and around eyes
    » Repeat same movements, keeping contact with skin at all times

11. Remove cleanser with warm, wet gauze:
    » Remove excess water from gauze
    » Start at upper chest; work upward and outward; use hand-over-hand strokes over neck
    » Use both sides of gauze pads or replace as needed
    » Avoid dragging or pulling skin

COMPLETION

» You are now ready to analyze the skin.

2 minutes Commercially Accepted Time

My Speed

INSTRUCTIONS:
Record your time in comparison with the commercially accepted time. Then list here how you could improve your performance.

SKIN ANALYSIS
SKILLS WORKSHOP

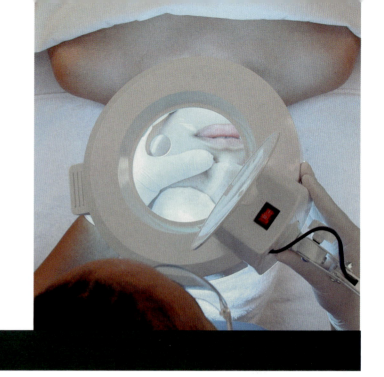

EXPLORE
Have you ever tried to bake without following a recipe?

INSPIRE
Performing a thorough skin analysis helps your client reach their skin care goals and sets the stage for a successful facial treatment.

ACHIEVE
Following this *Skin Analysis Skills Workshop*, you'll be able to:

» Demonstrate the proper skills to perform a facial skin analysis

PRODUCTS, TOOLS AND SUPPLIES:

PERFORMANCE GUIDE
SKIN ANALYSIS SKILLS
View the video, then practice the Skin Analysis procedure. Complete the self-check as you progress.

10 minutes Commercially Accepted Time

PREPARATION

Wash and dry your hands:
- Apply hand sanitizer
- Apply gloves

Note: Esthetician wears appropriate PPE at all times. Follow *all* applicable guidelines from regulating agencies regarding health, safety, infection control and personal protective equipment to be worn.

Set up workstation, supplies, products and treatment table.

OBSERVE

Observe phase:
- Review client intake form or records from previous visit
- Note demographic information
- Identify client concerns
- Verbally confirm reason for receiving treatment
- Identify health factors that could affect treatment
- Verify daily medications
- Identify issues that may be a caution for treatment
- Review lifestyle factors

Prior to skin analysis:
- Client has been assisted onto table
- Client has been appropriately draped
- Client's makeup has been removed and skin has been pre-cleansed

ANALYZE

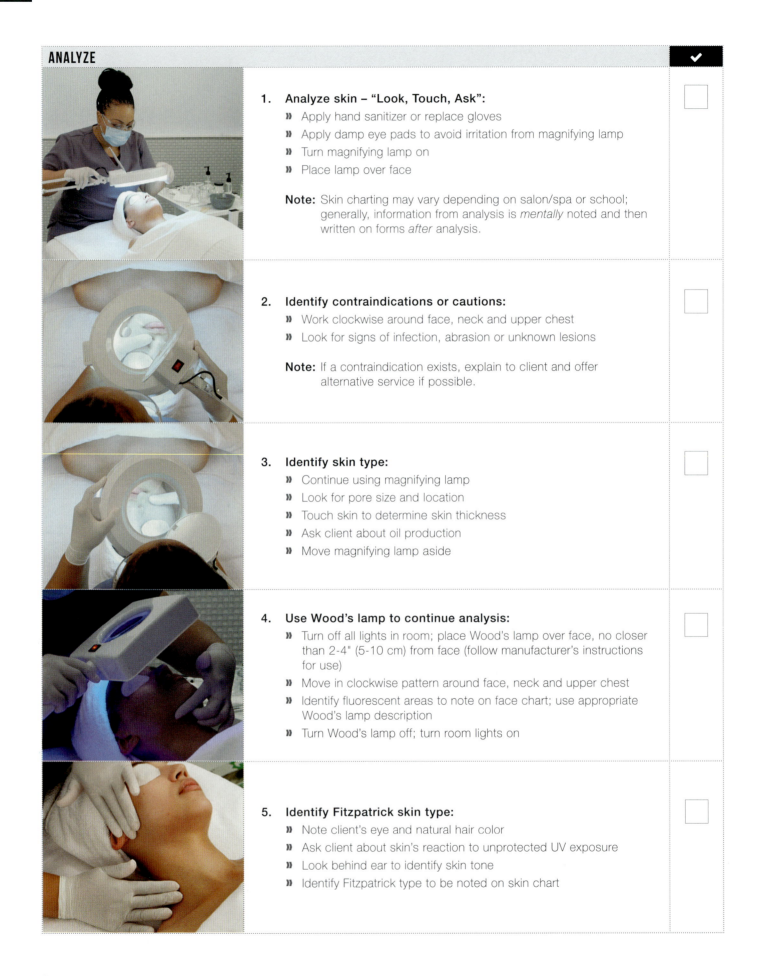

1. **Analyze skin – "Look, Touch, Ask":**
   - Apply hand sanitizer or replace gloves
   - Apply damp eye pads to avoid irritation from magnifying lamp
   - Turn magnifying lamp on
   - Place lamp over face

   Note: Skin charting may vary depending on salon/spa or school; generally, information from analysis is *mentally* noted and then written on forms *after* analysis.

2. **Identify contraindications or cautions:**
   - Work clockwise around face, neck and upper chest
   - Look for signs of infection, abrasion or unknown lesions

   Note: If a contraindication exists, explain to client and offer alternative service if possible.

3. **Identify skin type:**
   - Continue using magnifying lamp
   - Look for pore size and location
   - Touch skin to determine skin thickness
   - Ask client about oil production
   - Move magnifying lamp aside

4. **Use Wood's lamp to continue analysis:**
   - Turn off all lights in room; place Wood's lamp over face, no closer than 2-4" (5-10 cm) from face (follow manufacturer's instructions for use)
   - Move in clockwise pattern around face, neck and upper chest
   - Identify fluorescent areas to note on face chart; use appropriate Wood's lamp description
   - Turn Wood's lamp off; turn room lights on

5. **Identify Fitzpatrick skin type:**
   - Note client's eye and natural hair color
   - Ask client about skin's reaction to unprotected UV exposure
   - Look behind ear to identify skin tone
   - Identify Fitzpatrick type to be noted on skin chart

6. **Identify skin conditions using "Look" guidelines:**
   » Place magnifying lamp over face and turn on
   » Identify *color* characteristics looking for redness, gray/yellow, brown discoloration
   » Identify *structure* characteristics such as loose skin, broken capillaries, wrinkles, pustules, comedones, raised rough areas, flakiness

7. **Perform "Touch" tests:**
   » Determine if client has reactive skin, dehydration, elasticity issues, congestion, etc.
   » Run fingers over skin surface to test texture
   » Use pressure on various parts of the face to test sensitivity
   » Feel for unseen lesions

8. **Identify skin conditions using "Ask" guidelines:**
   » Turn off magnifying lamp and move it away from client; remove eye pads
   » Further verify answers from client intake form
   » Ask questions related to skin sensitivity, texture, sagging, aging, pigmentation and acne

9. **Create a summary analysis:**
   » Review and add notes to skin charting form summary area
   » Use face chart to note pore size/location and areas of skin conditions
   » Identify and note two specific skin condition categories to address
   » Determine products and tools to use for Increase, Balance and Decrease results

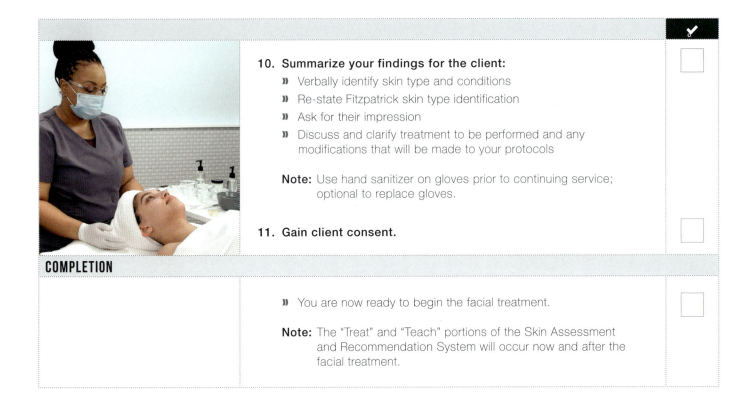

10. **Summarize your findings for the client:**
    » Verbally identify skin type and conditions
    » Re-state Fitzpatrick skin type identification
    » Ask for their impression
    » Discuss and clarify treatment to be performed and any modifications that will be made to your protocols

    Note: Use hand sanitizer on gloves prior to continuing service; optional to replace gloves.

11. **Gain client consent.**

COMPLETION

» You are now ready to begin the facial treatment.

Note: The "Treat" and "Teach" portions of the Skin Assessment and Recommendation System will occur now and after the facial treatment.

10 minutes Commercially Accepted Time

My Speed

INSTRUCTIONS:
Record your time in comparison with the commercially accepted time. Then list here how you could improve your performance.

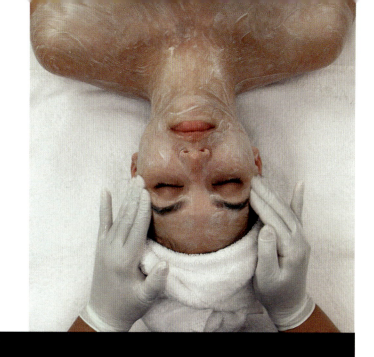

CLEANSE AND TONE
SKILLS WORKSHOP

EXPLORE
Have you ever washed your face but felt that it wasn't really clean when you finished, so you washed it a second time?

INSPIRE
Performing a second cleanse removes remaining dirt and impurities, increases microcirculation and prepares the skin for the remaining steps of the facial treatment.

ACHIEVE
Following this *Cleanse and Tone Skills Workshop*, you'll be able to:

» Demonstrate the proper skills to perform a facial cleanse and tone

PRODUCTS, TOOLS AND SUPPLIES:

_____
_____
_____
_____
_____
_____
_____
_____
_____
_____
_____

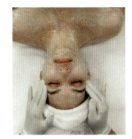

PERFORMANCE GUIDE
CLEANSE AND TONE SKILLS
View the video, then practice the Cleanse and Tone procedure. Complete the self-check as you progress.

3 minutes
Commercially Accepted Time

PREPARATION

Wash and dry your hands:
» Apply hand sanitizer
» Apply gloves

Note: Esthetician wears appropriate PPE at all times. Follow *all* applicable guidelines from regulating agencies regarding health, safety, infection control and personal protective equipment to be worn.

Set up workstation, supplies, products and treatment table.

Prior to cleanse and tone:
» Client has been assisted onto table
» Client has been appropriately draped
» Pre-cleanse has occurred
» Client's skin analysis has taken place

Note: The second cleanse is usually slightly longer than the first cleanse, with slower movements and medium pressure.

CLEANSE

1. **Obtain previously dispensed cleanser:**
   » Cleanser chosen for client's specific skin needs
   » Dispense amount based on manufacturer's recommendations

FACIAL TREATMENTS

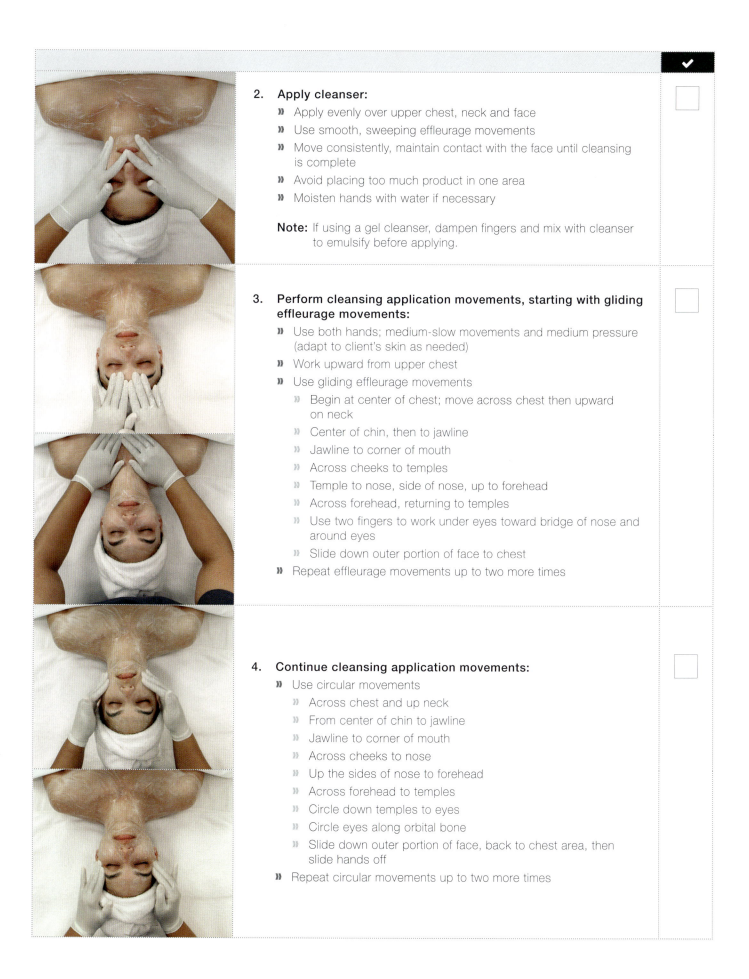

2. **Apply cleanser:**
   » Apply evenly over upper chest, neck and face
   » Use smooth, sweeping effleurage movements
   » Move consistently, maintain contact with the face until cleansing is complete
   » Avoid placing too much product in one area
   » Moisten hands with water if necessary

   Note: If using a gel cleanser, dampen fingers and mix with cleanser to emulsify before applying.

3. **Perform cleansing application movements, starting with gliding effleurage movements:**
   » Use both hands; medium-slow movements and medium pressure (adapt to client's skin as needed)
   » Work upward from upper chest
   » Use gliding effleurage movements
      » Begin at center of chest; move across chest then upward on neck
      » Center of chin, then to jawline
      » Jawline to corner of mouth
      » Across cheeks to temples
      » Temple to nose, side of nose, up to forehead
      » Across forehead, returning to temples
      » Use two fingers to work under eyes toward bridge of nose and around eyes
      » Slide down outer portion of face to chest
   » Repeat effleurage movements up to two more times

4. **Continue cleansing application movements:**
   » Use circular movements
      » Across chest and up neck
      » From center of chin to jawline
      » Jawline to corner of mouth
      » Across cheeks to nose
      » Up the sides of nose to forehead
      » Across forehead to temples
      » Circle down temples to eyes
      » Circle eyes along orbital bone
      » Slide down outer portion of face, back to chest area, then slide hands off
   » Repeat circular movements up to two more times

TONE

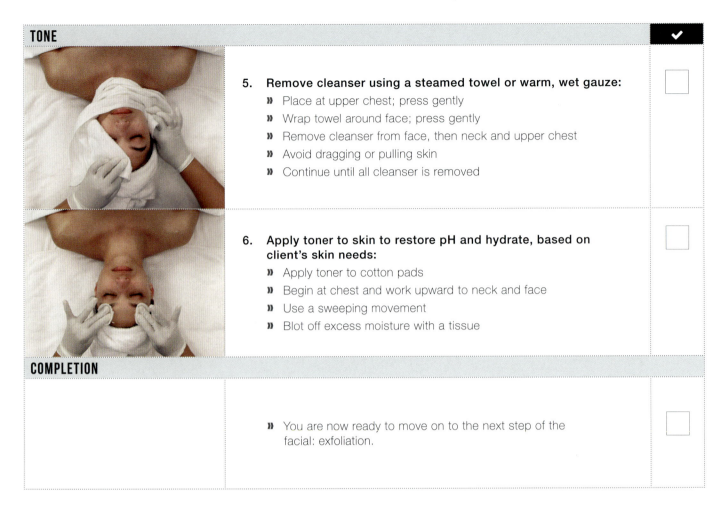

5. **Remove cleanser using a steamed towel or warm, wet gauze:**
   - Place at upper chest; press gently
   - Wrap towel around face; press gently
   - Remove cleanser from face, then neck and upper chest
   - Avoid dragging or pulling skin
   - Continue until all cleanser is removed

6. **Apply toner to skin to restore pH and hydrate, based on client's skin needs:**
   - Apply toner to cotton pads
   - Begin at chest and work upward to neck and face
   - Use a sweeping movement
   - Blot off excess moisture with a tissue

COMPLETION

- You are now ready to move on to the next step of the facial: exfoliation.

3 minutes Commercially Accepted Time

My Speed
_____
_____
_____

INSTRUCTIONS:
Record your time in comparison with the commercially accepted time. Then list here how you could improve your performance.

_____
_____
_____
_____
_____

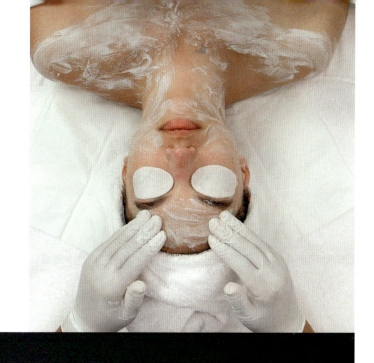

MECHANICAL EXFOLIATION AND EXTRACTION
SKILLS WORKSHOP

EXPLORE
Did you ever have to prepare a surface and remove imperfections so that it would accept a paint or stain effectively?

INSPIRE

During a facial treatment, exfoliation removes dead skin cells and debris for better product absorption and increased cell renewal. Extracting comedones safely and comfortably helps clients have clearer, more blemish-free skin.

ACHIEVE

Following this *Mechanical Exfoliation and Extraction Skills Workshop*, you'll be able to:

» Demonstrate the proper skills to perform a mechanical exfoliation

» Demonstrate proper skills to perform comedone extractions

PRODUCTS, TOOLS AND SUPPLIES:

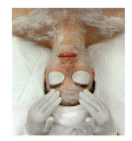

PERFORMANCE GUIDE
MECHANICAL EXFOLIATION AND EXTRACTION SKILLS

View the video, then practice the Mechanical Exfoliation and Extraction procedure. Complete the self-check as you progress.

10 minutes Commercially Accepted Time

PREPARATION

Wash and dry your hands:
» Apply hand sanitizer
» Apply gloves

Note: Esthetician wears appropriate PPE at all times. Follow *all* applicable guidelines from regulating agencies regarding health, safety, infection control and personal protective equipment to be worn.

Set up workstation, supplies, products and treatment table.

Prior to exfoliation:
» Client has been assisted to table
» Client has been appropriately draped
» Pre-cleanse, skin analysis, second cleanse and tone have occurred

MECHANICAL EXFOLIATION

1. **Turn on steamer:**
   » Position steamer arm away from client's head
   » Apply eye pads
   » Place tissue on either side of client's head

   Note: Do not use a steam application if it is contraindicated on the client's skin charting, e.g., sensitive skin types.

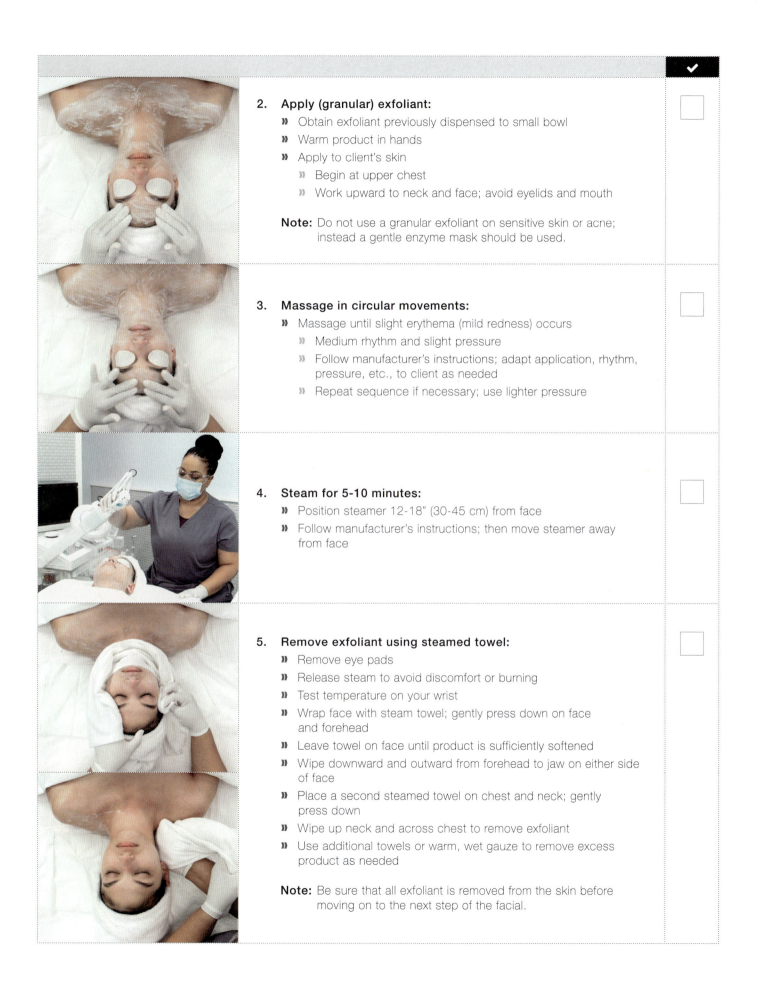

2. **Apply (granular) exfoliant:**
   - Obtain exfoliant previously dispensed to small bowl
   - Warm product in hands
   - Apply to client's skin
     - Begin at upper chest
     - Work upward to neck and face; avoid eyelids and mouth

   Note: Do not use a granular exfoliant on sensitive skin or acne; instead a gentle enzyme mask should be used.

3. **Massage in circular movements:**
   - Massage until slight erythema (mild redness) occurs
     - Medium rhythm and slight pressure
     - Follow manufacturer's instructions; adapt application, rhythm, pressure, etc., to client as needed
     - Repeat sequence if necessary; use lighter pressure

4. **Steam for 5-10 minutes:**
   - Position steamer 12-18" (30-45 cm) from face
   - Follow manufacturer's instructions; then move steamer away from face

5. **Remove exfoliant using steamed towel:**
   - Remove eye pads
   - Release steam to avoid discomfort or burning
   - Test temperature on your wrist
   - Wrap face with steam towel; gently press down on face and forehead
   - Leave towel on face until product is sufficiently softened
   - Wipe downward and outward from forehead to jaw on either side of face
   - Place a second steamed towel on chest and neck; gently press down
   - Wipe up neck and across chest to remove exfoliant
   - Use additional towels or warm, wet gauze to remove excess product as needed

   Note: Be sure that all exfoliant is removed from the skin before moving on to the next step of the facial.

EXTRACTION

6. **Perform extractions on comedones using finger-extraction method:**
   - Replace eye pads
   - Apply a thin layer of desincrustation solution using a fan brush
   - Apply only to clogged areas

7. **Steam for 3 minutes:**
   - Remove steamer and turn off

8. **Perform extraction:**
   - Position magnifying lamp over face no closer than 1-2" (2.5-5 cm)
   - Wrap gauze pads moistened with astringent or desincrustation solution around index fingers
   - Place index finger on each side of the comedone
   - Press down around the comedone
     - Lift skin under the comedone and gently compress skin, moving slightly back-and-forth in a rocking motion
   - Repeat extractions as needed
   - Move lamp (or leave in place to apply astringent)

   Note: Do not perform extractions for more than 5 minutes.

9. **Blot with astringent to kill bacteria:**
   - Do not force sebum out of skin; be gentle
   - Do not use fingernails or other sharp instruments

   Note: If breakouts are present, apply an antibacterial product to those areas then apply treatment serum.

10. **Use a comedone extractor if allowed by regulating agency:**
    - Move the extractor gently back and forth, and from side to side until comedone is released
    - Wipe extracted comedone onto gauze pad

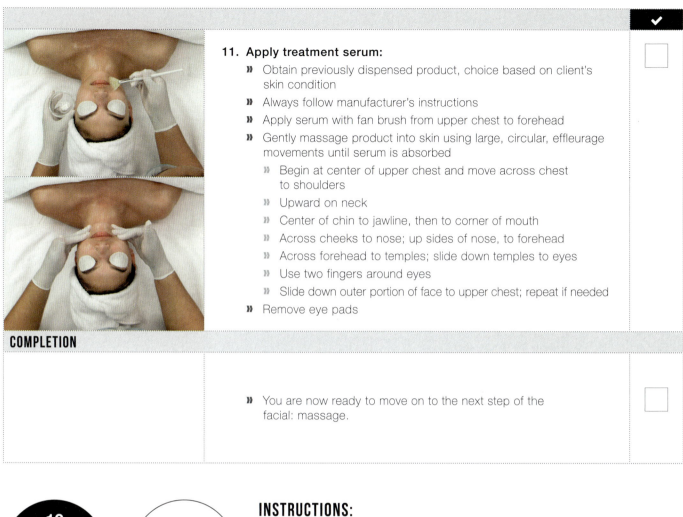

11. **Apply treatment serum:**
    » Obtain previously dispensed product, choice based on client's skin condition
    » Always follow manufacturer's instructions
    » Apply serum with fan brush from upper chest to forehead
    » Gently massage product into skin using large, circular, effleurage movements until serum is absorbed
        » Begin at center of upper chest and move across chest to shoulders
        » Upward on neck
        » Center of chin to jawline, then to corner of mouth
        » Across cheeks to nose; up sides of nose, to forehead
        » Across forehead to temples; slide down temples to eyes
        » Use two fingers around eyes
        » Slide down outer portion of face to upper chest; repeat if needed
    » Remove eye pads

COMPLETION

» You are now ready to move on to the next step of the facial: massage.

10 minutes Commercially Accepted Time

My Speed

INSTRUCTIONS:
Record your time in comparison with the commercially accepted time. Then list here how you could improve your performance.

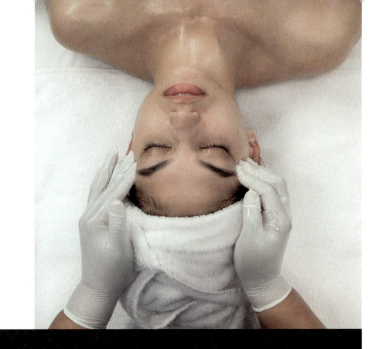

MASSAGE
SKILLS WORKSHOP

EXPLORE
Why do you think many clients say that the massage is their favorite part of a facial treatment?

INSPIRE
The massage techniques you perform benefit the client's skin and are the most relaxing and enjoyable part of the facial treatment.

ACHIEVE
Following this *Massage Skills Workshop*, you'll be able to:

» Demonstrate the proper skills to perform a facial massage

PRODUCTS, TOOLS AND SUPPLIES:

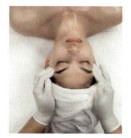

PERFORMANCE GUIDE

MASSAGE SKILLS

View the video, then practice the Massage procedure. Complete the self-check as you progress.

10 minutes
Commercially Accepted Time

PREPARATION	✓

Wash and dry your hands:
» Apply hand sanitizer
» Apply gloves

Note: Esthetician wears appropriate PPE at all times. Follow *all* applicable guidelines from regulating agencies regarding health, safety, infection control and personal protective equipment to be worn.

Set up workstation, supplies, products and treatment table.

Prior to application of mask and protection:
» Client has been assisted to table
» Client has been appropriately draped
» Pre-cleanse, skin analysis, second cleanse, tone, exfoliation, extraction and treatment serum application steps have been performed

APPLY MASSAGE MEDIUM

Obtain appropriate, previously dispensed massage medium (cream, oil, gel) based on skin type and condition:
» Determine amount based on:
  » Manufacturer's recommendations
  » Area to be covered
  » Amount of "slip" desired for massage

PIVOT POINT FUNDAMENTALS: ESTHETICS | 107ᴱ.10 - 115

Apply massage medium:
- Warm product in hands if not warm
- Apply over upper chest, neck and face
- Use slow rhythm and light pressure to apply

Note: During massage, work in appropriate rhythm and use appropriate pressure for the client.

MASSAGE

Note: Solid overlays indicate that the massage movement is performed on the front side. Dashed overlays indicate the massage movement is performed behind the shoulders.

1. Place fingertips of both hands at top of sternum, have client take a deep breath.

2. Perform large circular movements using both hands:
   - Across upper chest
   - Around shoulders
   - Up trapezius to base of neck

3. Perform thumb-kneading movements, with both hands, on sides of posterior neck to occipital.

4. Hold occipital with both hands:
   - Gently stretch neck for 10 seconds
   - Slide hands back to upper chest

   Note: If client has neck injury, omit this step.

5. **Work out to the shoulders, then use thumb-kneading movements:**
   » Move along the trapezius, working up the neck

6. **Slide hands back to upper chest:**
   » Repeat once (steps 1-6)

7. **Perform long, sweeping, hand-over-hand movements from the upper chest to jawline:**
   » Repeat twice

8. **Slide both hands to base of skull.**

9. **Using both hands, gently turn the client's head to the side and use large, circular, kneading movements up the trapezius, then the sternocleidomastoid, ending at the ear:**
   » Slide back to base of skull

10. **Repeat on other side:**
    » Then slide both hands to upper chest

11. **Perform fast windmill movements with both hands:**
    » Move up neck
    » Move across jawline in both directions
    » Repeat twice then stop on chin

12. **Apply pressure at the center of the chin.**

13. **Perform small circular movements with both hands back and forth along jawline:**
    » End at corners of mouth

14. **Perform scissor movements with alternating hands on mouth and chin:**
    » Repeat twice

15. **Slide to cheeks, perform pull-up-and-hold movement on cheeks with both hands:**
    » Then slide to chin

16. **Perform small circular movements with fingertips of both hands:**
    » Begin at chin and work up cheeks

17. **Slide to corrugator, then perform scissor movements with alternating hands:**
    » Upward on nose
    » Then slide down sides of nose

18. **Perform small circular movements at outer corner of nose:**
    » Move up side of nose, around eyes and back to nose

19. **Perform figure-eight movements around eyes:**
    » Repeat six times
    » Then slide to temples

20. **Perform small circular movements around temples with both hands:**
    » Pause at temples and apply pressure

21. **Perform tapping movement around eyes:**
    » Move in circle outside of eyes with ring and index fingers

22. **Slide to temples, perform a pressure point movement:**
    » Slide right hand over to left

23. **Perform half-circle movements back and forth across forehead:**
    » Repeat

24. **Perform a sweeping hand-over-hand movement at forehead:**
    » Repeat

25. **Perform 4-finger interlock glide movement across forehead:**
    » Repeat twice

26. **Slide down sides of face to earlobes and gently pull off:**
    » Remove excess massage medium if necessary:
        » Use steamed towel or warm, wet gauze
        » Light, upward movements

COMPLETION

» You are now ready to move on to the mask and protect step of the facial treatment.

10 minutes
Commercially Accepted Time

My Speed

INSTRUCTIONS:
Record your time in comparison with the commercially accepted time.
Then list here how you could improve your performance.

MASK AND PROTECT
SKILLS WORKSHOP

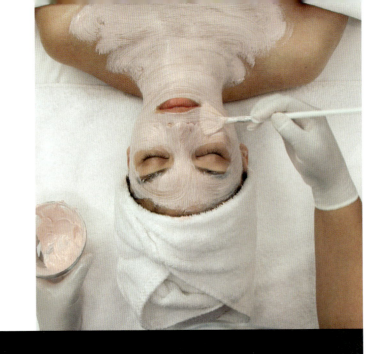

EXPLORE
Have you ever left a facial appointment and wished your skin looked and felt better?

INSPIRE
Applying a facial mask and appropriate protection products will calm the skin, leaving it moisturized and well-protected.

ACHIEVE
Following this *Mask and Protect Skills Workshop*, you'll be able to:

» Demonstrate the proper skills to perform a facial mask and protection

PRODUCTS, TOOLS AND SUPPLIES:

PERFORMANCE GUIDE

MASK AND PROTECT SKILLS

View the video, then practice the Mask and Protect procedure. Complete the self-check as you progress.

18 minutes
Commercially Accepted Time

PREPARATION

Wash and dry your hands:
- Apply hand sanitizer
- Apply gloves

Note: Esthetician wears appropriate PPE at all times. Follow *all* applicable guidelines from regulating agencies regarding health, safety, infection control and personal protective equipment to be worn.

Set up workstation, supplies, products and treatment table.

Prior to application of mask and protection:
- Client has been assisted to table
- Client has been appropriately draped
- Pre-cleanse, skin analysis, second cleanse and tone, exfoliation and extraction, and massage have occurred

MASK

1. **Obtain mask:**
   - Apply gloves
   - Apply eye pads
   - Obtain mask and fan brush

   Note: If cream mask is being used and can be applied around the orbital bone (avoiding the eye lids), eye pads may be applied after the mask application.

2. **Apply mask using fan brush and long, sweeping strokes:**
   - Begin application at upper chest
   - Work upward
   - Work across neck and chin

3. **Continue mask application on face:**
   - Work up cheeks using long, slow strokes
   - Cover entire area, including upper lip
   - Apply mask to nose, forehead and around eyes

   Note: Use multiple mask products, if necessary, to address client skin needs.

4. **Reapply as needed to ensure complete coverage:**
   - Apply eye pads

5. **Allow mask to set for required time:**
   - 5-10 minutes or according to manufacturer's instructions

6. **Apply steamed towel:**
   - Remove two steamed towels from cabinet
   - Release steam from towels
   - Test temperature before applying
   - Apply one towel across chest
   - Apply second towel around face

   Note: Always leave nostrils and mouth uncovered when steam wrapping.

7. **Remove mask:**
   - Gently press down on chest, face and forehead
   - Remove eye pads
   - Wipe from forehead to jaw using downward and outward strokes
   - Wipe upward on neck
   - Wipe across upper chest and shoulders

   Note: If necessary, use more towels or warm, wet gauze to remove excess mask product (more likely with a clay mask); be certain that all product is removed before continuing with the service.

8. **Apply toner:**
   - Begin at upper chest and work toward forehead
   - Avoid excess product

PROTECT

9. **Apply eye cream:**
   - Obtain previously dispensed eye cream
   - Apply with pads of fingers using small tapping motions around eyes

   Note: Light circular movements can also be used around eyes.

10. **Apply serum:**
    - Obtain previously dispensed serum
    - Apply to upper chest, neck and face
    - Use product application movements (effleurage) with light pressure, working upward and outward

11. **Apply moisturizer:**
    - Obtain previously dispensed moisturizer
    - Apply moisturizer to upper chest, neck and face
    - Same effleurage movements, pressure and directions

12. **Apply sun protection:**
    - Obtain previously dispensed sun protection product
    - Apply to upper chest, neck and face
    - Same movements, pressure and directions
    - Use an SPF of 30 or higher

COMPLETION

- This completes the *Mask and Protect Skills* workshop. If this were part of a full facial service, you would now move on to complete the service.

18 minutes Commercially Accepted Time

My Speed

INSTRUCTIONS:
Record your time in comparison with the commercially accepted time. Then list here how you could improve your performance.

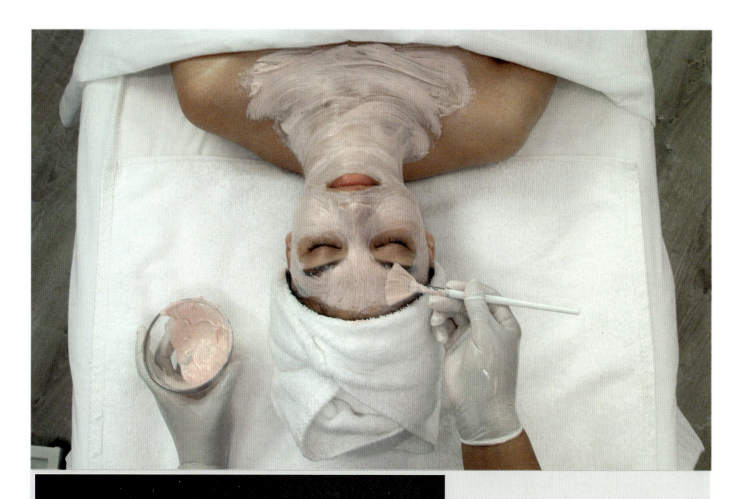

BASIC FACIAL TREATMENT

EXPLORE
What makes a basic facial treatment valuable to clients so they return regularly?

INSPIRE
Customizing a facial treatment to the client's unique needs will ensure return visits and referrals.

ACHIEVE
Following this *Basic Facial Treatment Workshop*, you'll be able to:

» Demonstrate proper procedures to perform a basic facial treatment

» Adapt the basic facial treatment based on the skin analysis and individual client needs

BASIC FACIAL TREATMENT PROCEDURES

	TOOLS/SUPPLIES	PRODUCTS
1. PRE-CLEANSE:		Hand Sanitizer, Makeup Remover, Cleanser
2. ANALYZE:		
3. CLEANSE AND TONE:		Cleanser, Toner
4. EXFOLIATE:		Exfoliant
5. TREAT:	(Optional)	Desincrustation Solution, Toner, Serum
6. MASSAGE	N/A	Massage Medium

FACIAL TREATMENTS

BASIC FACIAL TREATMENT PROCEDURES (CONT'D)

	TOOLS/SUPPLIES	PRODUCTS
7. MASK		Mask, Toner
8. PROTECT	N/A	Eye Cream, Moisturizer, Sun Protection, Serum

PERFORMANCE GUIDE
BASIC FACIAL TREATMENT
View the video, then practice the Basic Facial Treatment procedure. Complete the self-check as you progress.

60 minutes
Commercially Accepted Time

PREPARATION

Wash your hands:
» Apply hand sanitizer
» Apply gloves

Note: Esthetician wears appropriate PPE at all times. Follow all applicable guidelines from regulating agencies regarding health, safety, infection control and personal protective equipment to be worn.

Set up workstation and treatment table following regulatory guidelines:
» Layered treatment-table setup

Place fresh wet towels in hot-towel cabinet:
» Calming aromatherapy oils were used

Perform Observe steps in the Skin Assessment and Recommendation System:
» Review client record
» Identify contraindications and cautions
» Ask about skin concerns
» Review lifestyle and health factors

Note: The client intake form and health history should be filled out before the appointment.

PRE-CLEANSE

1. Wash hands and apply gloves or apply hand sanitizer to gloves if already on.

2. Drape/cover client appropriately.

3. Perform makeup removal:
   » Choose makeup remover for all skin types

4. Perform superficial cleanse (1st cleanse):
   » Choose cleanser suitable for all skin types unless you can determine client-specific product
   » Apply cleanser evenly over upper chest, neck, and face
   » Use cleansing application movements following manufacturer's recommendations (generally light pressure and fast speed)
   » Remove with warm, wet towel or gauze; discard after use

   🌐 For this client, a gentle hydrating cleanser is used for the superficial cleanse with light pressure and fast movements.

ANALYZE

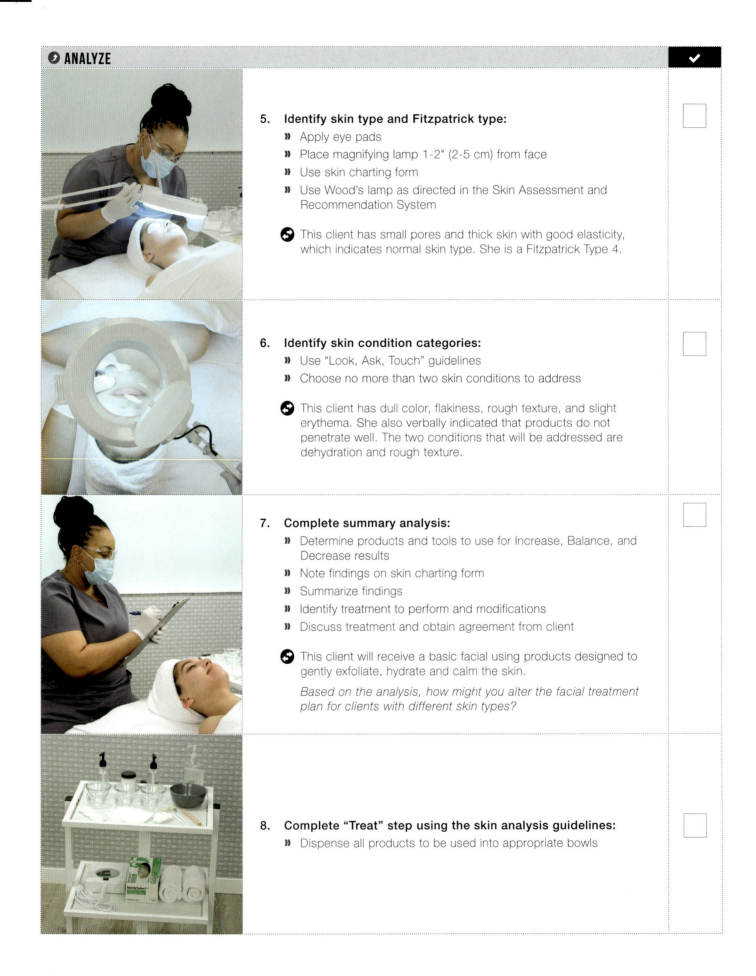

5. **Identify skin type and Fitzpatrick type:**
   - Apply eye pads
   - Place magnifying lamp 1-2" (2-5 cm) from face
   - Use skin charting form
   - Use Wood's lamp as directed in the Skin Assessment and Recommendation System

   ⊕ This client has small pores and thick skin with good elasticity, which indicates normal skin type. She is a Fitzpatrick Type 4.

6. **Identify skin condition categories:**
   - Use "Look, Ask, Touch" guidelines
   - Choose no more than two skin conditions to address

   ⊕ This client has dull color, flakiness, rough texture, and slight erythema. She also verbally indicated that products do not penetrate well. The two conditions that will be addressed are dehydration and rough texture.

7. **Complete summary analysis:**
   - Determine products and tools to use for Increase, Balance, and Decrease results
   - Note findings on skin charting form
   - Summarize findings
   - Identify treatment to perform and modifications
   - Discuss treatment and obtain agreement from client

   ⊕ This client will receive a basic facial using products designed to gently exfoliate, hydrate and calm the skin.

   Based on the analysis, how might you alter the facial treatment plan for clients with different skin types?

8. **Complete "Treat" step using the skin analysis guidelines:**
   - Dispense all products to be used into appropriate bowls

FACIAL TREATMENTS

CLEANSE AND TONE

9. **Apply cleanser evenly over upper chest, neck and face (2nd cleanse):**
   - Use appropriate pressure for client
   - Be consistent, remain in contact with face until cleansing is complete

   ↻ A gentle hydrating cleanser is used for this client; if using a gel cleanser, emulsify first then apply.

10. **Perform cleansing application movements:**
    - Use both hands and appropriate pressure for a deep or 2nd cleanse
    - Work upward from upper chest
    - Use sliding effleurage movements; repeat effleurage movements three times
    - Use circular movements; repeat circular movements three times

    Note: Medium pressure and standard medium-slow movements are used; speed should increase with repetition; obtain additional cleanser and water if needed.

11. **Remove cleanser using a steamed towel or warm, wet gauze:**
    - If using towels, always check the temperature and be especially cautious if client has sensitive skin
    - Make sure all cleanser is removed from skin

12. **Apply toner:**
    - Choose toner based on skin analysis
    - Blot off excess moisture with tissue

    ↻ A hydrating toner has been chosen for this client.

EXFOLIATE

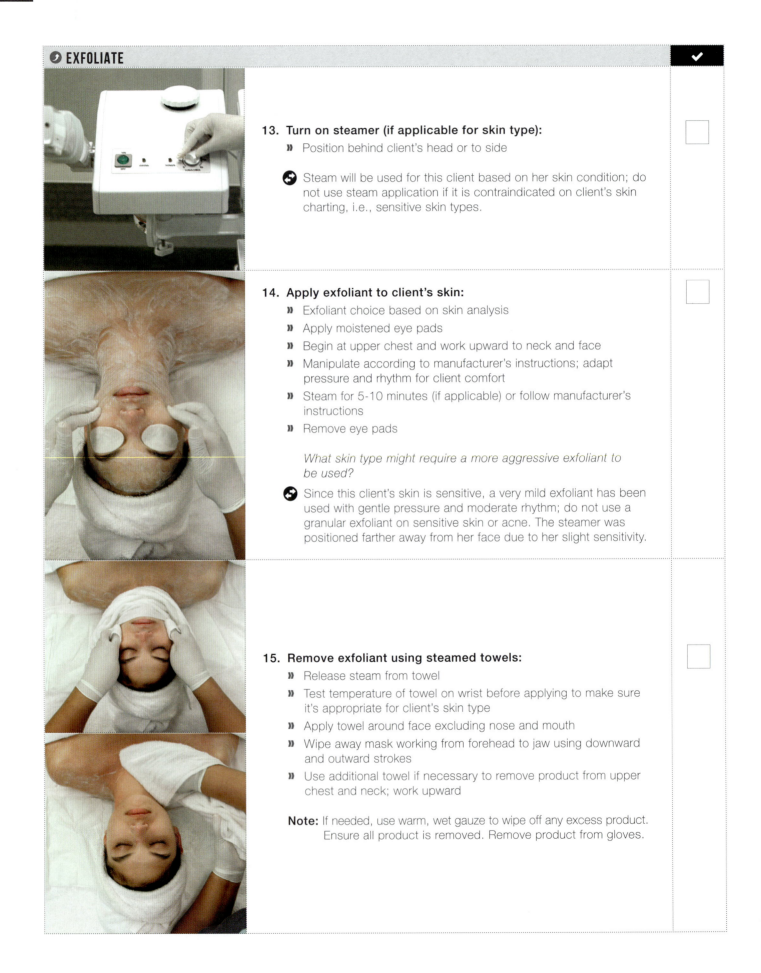

13. Turn on steamer (if applicable for skin type):
- Position behind client's head or to side

🌐 Steam will be used for this client based on her skin condition; do not use steam application if it is contraindicated on client's skin charting, i.e., sensitive skin types.

14. Apply exfoliant to client's skin:
- Exfoliant choice based on skin analysis
- Apply moistened eye pads
- Begin at upper chest and work upward to neck and face
- Manipulate according to manufacturer's instructions; adapt pressure and rhythm for client comfort
- Steam for 5-10 minutes (if applicable) or follow manufacturer's instructions
- Remove eye pads

What skin type might require a more aggressive exfoliant to be used?

🌐 Since this client's skin is sensitive, a very mild exfoliant has been used with gentle pressure and moderate rhythm; do not use a granular exfoliant on sensitive skin or acne. The steamer was positioned farther away from her face due to her slight sensitivity.

15. Remove exfoliant using steamed towels:
- Release steam from towel
- Test temperature of towel on wrist before applying to make sure it's appropriate for client's skin type
- Apply towel around face excluding nose and mouth
- Wipe away mask working from forehead to jaw using downward and outward strokes
- Use additional towel if necessary to remove product from upper chest and neck; work upward

Note: If needed, use warm, wet gauze to wipe off any excess product. Ensure all product is removed. Remove product from gloves.

TREAT

16. Perform extractions on comedones using finger extraction method:
- Apply eye pads
- Apply a thin layer of desincrustation solution to clogged areas
- Position steamer 12-18" (30-45 cm) from face
- Steam for three minutes at appropriate distance based on skin type and solution used; turn off steamer
- Position magnifying lamp over face, no closer than 1-2" (2.5-5 cm)
- Carefully perform extraction
- Watch for skin irritation
- Immediately blot with astringent to kill bacteria
- Change gauze pad if pads dry out or become filled with debris

Note: Desincrustation solutions are generally suited for all skin types; cotton swabs can be used instead of fingers wrapped in gauze.

17. Apply treatment serum using fan brush:
- Serum choice based on skin analysis
- Use large, circular effleurage movements to massage until serum is absorbed in skin

➲ A light, hydrating serum is used for this client, applied with light pressure and a medium rhythm.

MASSAGE

18. Apply massage medium using product application movements:
- Product choice based on skin type and condition
- Adapt rhythm and pressure to suit client

➲ A lightweight hydrating cream to provide hydration is used for this client.

19. **Perform massage movements:**
    - » Massage face, neck, upper chest and shoulders using effleurage, petrissage, tapotement (percussion) and friction movements
    - » Refer to the massage movements chart in the *Facial Treatment Skills* lesson
    - » Remove excess massage medium with wet gauze and light, upward movements if needed

    🔄 Medium pressure and rhythm are used for this client.

    How would you adapt massage rhythm or pressure for a client with more sensitive skin?

MASK

20. **Apply mask:**
    - » Mask choice based on skin analysis
    - » Use a fan brush with long, sweeping strokes
    - » Use more than one mask if required for client's skin condition
    - » Apply eye pads
    - » Allow mask to set on face for required time indicated by manufacturer (usually 10-20 minutes)

    🔄 A hydrating cream mask is used for this client; use multiple mask types if needed for the client's skin condition.

    What skin types might lead you to choose a different kind of mask?

21. **Remove mask with steamed towel and warm, wet gauze if necessary.**

    Note: You may need to use more towels or gauze to wipe away excess mask product. Be sure all mask product is removed before moving forward.

22. **Apply appropriate toner.**

    🔄 A hydrating toner is used.

● PROTECT

23. **Apply appropriate eye cream for client's skin condition:**
    - » Perform light, pressing, tapping motions around eyes working outward from inner corners of eyes; use ring finger for gentle application
    - 🌐 A hydrating and calming anti-wrinkle cream is used for this client.

24. **Apply appropriate serum, moisturizer and sun protection over chest, neck and face:**
    - » Use effleurage movements from neck to forehead, stroking upward and outward
    - » Use an SPF 15 or higher
    - 🌐 A hydrating serum was chosen for this client along with a calming, balanced moisturizing cream.

COMPLETION

- » Complete the "Teach" phase of the Skin Assessment and Recommendation System
- » Include written after-care instructions that outline specific products to use within 48 hours, and lifestyle cautions such as avoiding heat and sun exposure
- » Discard single-use supplies
- » Disinfect tools and multi-use supplies
- » Disinfect workstation and arrange in proper order
- » Place used towels in a closed container or place in washing machine
- » Change treatment-table linens to prepare for next client

60 minutes Commercially Accepted Time

My Speed

INSTRUCTIONS:
Record your time in comparison with the commercially accepted time. Then list here how you could improve your performance.

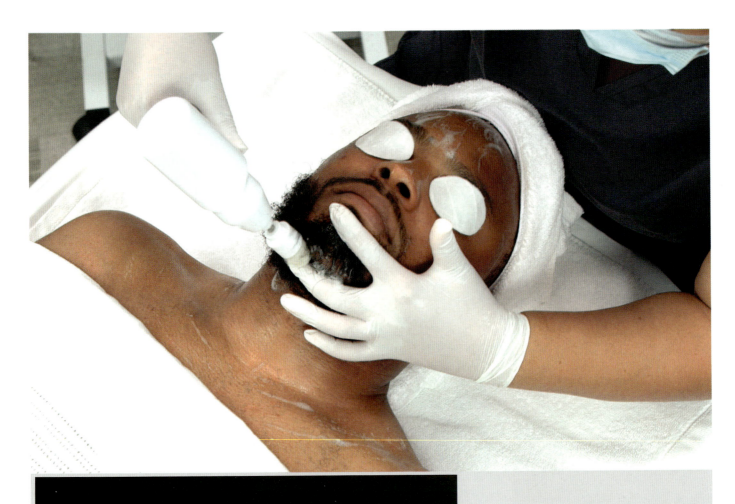

MEN'S FACIAL TREATMENT

EXPLORE

What do you think might be a challenge with performing a facial on a male client that you may not experience on a female client?

INSPIRE

With more men increasingly seeking skin care services, an esthetician who provides a comfortable experience for a male client while helping him reach his skin care goals is invaluable.

ACHIEVE

Following this *Men's Facial Treatment Workshop*, you'll be able to:

» Demonstrate proper procedures to perform a men's facial treatment

» Adapt the facial treatment based on the skin analysis and the unique needs of the male client

MEN'S FACIAL TREATMENT PROCEDURES

	TOOLS/SUPPLIES/DEVICES	PRODUCTS
1. PRE-CLEANSE:		Hand Sanitizer, Makeup Remover, Cleanser
2. ANALYZE:		
3. CLEANSE AND TONE:		Cleanser, Toner
4. EXFOLIATE:		Exfoliant
5. TREAT:	(Optional)	Desincrustation Solution, Toner, Serum
6. MASSAGE	N/A	Massage Medium

MEN'S FACIAL TREATMENT PROCEDURES (CONT'D)

	TOOLS/SUPPLIES	PRODUCTS
7. MASK		Mask, Toner, Massage Medium
8. PROTECT	N/A	Eye Cream, Moisturizer, Sun Protection, Serum

PERFORMANCE GUIDE
MEN'S FACIAL TREATMENT

View the video, then practice the Men's Facial Treatment procedure. Complete the self-check as you progress.

60 minutes Commercially Accepted Time

PREPARATION		✓
	Wash your hands: » Apply hand sanitizer » Apply gloves **Note: Esthetician wears appropriate PPE at all times.** Follow all applicable guidelines from regulating agencies regarding health, safety, infection control and personal protective equipment to be worn.	☐
	Set up workstation and treatment table following regulatory guidelines: » Layered treatment-table setup	☐
	Place fresh wet towels in hot-towel cabinet: » Add sandalwood essential oil to the towels	☐
	Perform Observe steps in the Skin Assessment and Recommendation System: » Review client record » Identify contraindications and cautions » Ask about skin concerns » Review lifestyle and health factors **Note:** The client intake form and health history should be filled out before the appointment.	☐

PRE-CLEANSE

1. Wash hands and apply gloves or apply hand sanitizer to gloves if already on.

2. Assist the client onto the treatment table and drape appropriately:
   » A rolled towel is placed under his neck

3. For pre-cleanse, apply cleanser from the upper chest, up toward the forehead:
   » Apply cleanser over facial hair area in a downward direction with grain of the hair

4. Use circular downward movements to cleanse the skin below the beard.

   If your client does not have a beard, or has a clean-shaven facial hair area, will you still need to use downward movements?

FACIAL TREATMENTS

5. **Remove the cleanser with warm towels instead of gauze or cotton pads to prevent it from clinging to the face:**
   » Use downward strokes when removing product in facial hair area

ANALYZE

6. **Analyze the skin using magnifying lamp and Wood's lamp.**

   Client analysis shows:
   » Medium to large pores throughout the face and thick skin
   » Wood's lamp shows small orange dots throughout the face, which indicates oily skin
   » Fitzpatrick Type 6, with a dull appearance, comedones and flakiness
   » Concerns to be addressed include:
      » Dehydration
      » Congested skin

CLEANSE AND TONE

7. **Apply gel cleanser and work into skin; use rotating brush device for additional cleansing and gentle exfoliation:**
   » Gel cleanser emulsified using fan brush
   » Small circular movements used to work cleanser into skin

   Why do you think a gel cleanser works well on men's skin?

8. **For beards over 1" in length, part the beard using two fingers to lift the hair:**
   » Place rotating brush to cleanse skin under beard

   Note: The rotating brush will be covered in the *Facial Treatment With Devices* area of study.

9. **Remove cleanser with a steamed towel:**
   » Use downward strokes to work with the grain of the hair

10. **Cleanse the neck and upper chest using the rotating brush:**
    » Move rotating brush using up-and-down movements
    » Move across upper chest from side to side
    » Remove cleanser using steamed towel

11. **As an alternative, the beard could be cleansed using your hands with downward strokes working from one side to the other.**

EXFOLIATE

12. **Apply enzyme exfoliant:**
    » Apply to neck first using long strokes, then areas above beard including eyes, nose, cheek and forehead
    » Avoid applying to beard area

    Note: If the face is freshly shaven or if the client has razor burn, no exfoliation is recommended on that area. Gel exfoliant is good to use in the beard area; avoid using thick creams.

13. **Apply steam to activate the enzyme exfoliant using manufacturer's instructions.**

FACIAL TREATMENTS

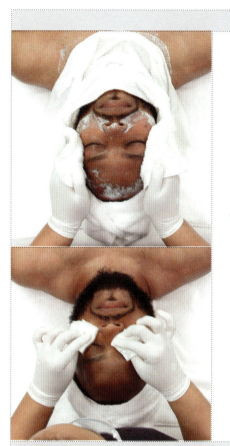

14. **Remove exfoliant:**
    » Use steamed towels as needed
    » Remove residual product using a moistened gauze pad

TREAT

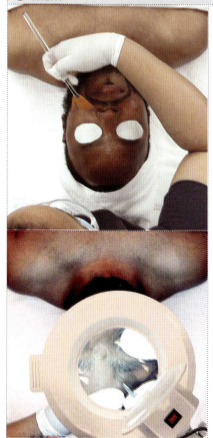

15. **After applying eye pads, apply desincrustation solution:**
    » Apply using a fan brush to all areas of congestion
    » Perform extractions; immediately apply astringent as you work
    » Apply astringent to entire face after extractions

    Note: Avoid trying to remove every comedone in the first treatment; doing so could damage the skin.

MASSAGE

16. Apply beard oil as a massage medium to the entire face:
- » Massage movements in facial hair area are performed in a downward, circular direction
- » Massage in direction of hair growth to prevent discomfort and possible ingrown hairs

MASK

17. Apply mask:
- » Use the usual application movements from upper chest up toward forehead
- » Apply over beard using downward strokes
- » Apply cotton eye pads
- » Remove mask using steamed towels; allow towel to sit over mask up to two minutes to loosen product

🌀 For this client a non-setting mask designed for dehydration is applied using the usual application movements from the upper chest up toward the forehead. The mask is applied over the beard using downward strokes.

Why do you think that a non-setting mask is used instead of a setting mask for this client?

18. Apply appropriate toner using gauze pads.

🌀 A balancing toner is used.

PROTECT

19. To protect the skin, apply lip cream, eye cream, serum, moisturizer and SPF using the appropriate procedures.

    Note: Gel is good to use in the beard area. Thick creams should be avoided.

COMPLETION

- Complete the 'Teach" phase of the Skin Assessment and Recommendation system
- Include written after-care instructions that outline specific products to use within 48 hours and lifestyle cautions such as avoiding heat and sun exposure
- Discard single-use supplies
- Disinfect tools and multi-use supplies
- Disinfect workstation and arrange in proper order
- Place used towels in a closed container or place in washing machine
- Change treatment table linens to prepare for next client

60 minutes Commercially Accepted Time

My Speed

INSTRUCTIONS:
Record your time in comparison with the commercially accepted time. Then list here how you could improve your performance.

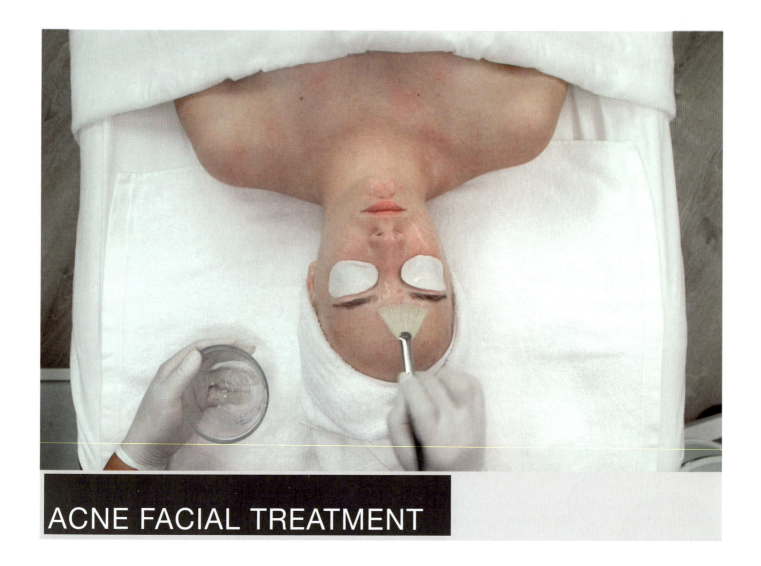

ACNE FACIAL TREATMENT

EXPLORE

What do you think is unique about an acne facial?

INSPIRE

Estheticians who are well-versed in delivering skin balancing treatments for clients with acneic skin can grow a significant clientele in salon/spas and also experience career growth in medical environments.

ACHIEVE

Following this *Acne Facial Treatment Workshop*, you'll be able to:

» Demonstrate proper procedures to perform an acne facial treatment

» Adapt the facial treatment based on the skin analysis and the unique needs of clients with oily, problematic skin

ACNE FACIAL TREATMENT PROCEDURES

	TOOLS/SUPPLIES	PRODUCTS
1. PRE-CLEANSE:	headband, cotton pads, tissues, gloves	Hand Sanitizer, Makeup Remover, Cleanser
2. ANALYZE:	cotton pads, magnifying lamp, Wood's lamp, gloves	
3. CLEANSE AND TONE:	tissues, cotton pads, tissue box, gloves	Cleanser, Toner
4. EXFOLIATE:	warm towel, steamer, cotton pads, tissues	Exfoliant
5. TREAT:	magnifying lamp, mask brush, cotton pads, gloves, tissues, extractor (Optional), tissue box	Desincrustation Solution, Toner, Serum
6. MASSAGE	N/A	Massage Medium

PIVOT POINT FUNDAMENTALS: ESTHETICS | 107E.14 - 149

ACNE FACIAL TREATMENT PROCEDURES (CONT'D)

	TOOLS/SUPPLIES	PRODUCTS
7. MASK		Mask, Toner, Massage Medium
8. PROTECT	N/A	Eye Cream, Moisturizer, Sun Protection, Serum

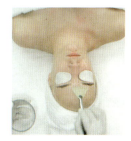

PERFORMANCE GUIDE
ACNE FACIAL TREATMENT

View the video, then practice the Acne Facial Treatment procedure. Complete the self-check as you progress.

60 minutes
Commercially Accepted Time

PREPARATION

Wash your hands:
- Apply hand sanitizer
- Apply gloves

Note: Esthetician wears appropriate PPE at all times. Follow all applicable guidelines from regulating agencies regarding health, safety, infection control and personal protective equipment to be worn.

Set up workstation and treatment table following regulatory guidelines:
- Layered treatment-table setup

Place fresh wet towels in hot-towel cabinet:
- Avoid adding essential oils to towels

Perform Observe steps in the Skin Assessment and Recommendation System:
- Review client record
- Identify contraindications and cautions
- Ask about skin concerns
- Review lifestyle and health factors

Note: The client intake form and health history should be filled out before the appointment.

PRE-CLEANSE

1. Wash hands and apply gloves or apply hand sanitizer to gloves if already on.

2. Assist the client onto the treatment table and drape appropriately.

3. For pre-cleanse, avoid using products designed for dry skin, which could clog pores on acneic skin:
   » Remove product using steamed towel

ANALYZE

4. Analyze the skin using magnifying lamp and Wood's lamp:
   » Look out for skin irritations or sensitivity

   Client analysis shows:
   » Medium to large pores throughout the face and thick skin
   » Wood's lamp shows small orange dots throughout the face and hairline: oily skin type
   » Fitzpatrick Type 1 – Avoid products that will cause sun sensitivity
   » Concerns to be addressed is grade 2 acne including:
      » Widespread comedones
      » Pustules
      » Flakiness

CLEANSE AND TONE

5. **Apply gel cleanser to address oily skin:**
   - Gel cleanser emulsified using fan brush
   - Use light, slow movements

6. **Remove cleanser with a steamed towel.**

EXFOLIATE

7. **Apply enzyme mask (exfoliant):**
   - Mix exfoliant in small bowl following manufacturer's instructions
   - Use long strokes working from upper chest toward forehead
   - Apply extra exfoliant to all areas of congestion discovered during skin analysis

   Which is more appropriate if client is experiencing sensitivity: steam or a moistened gauze?

8. **Apply steam or moistened gauze to keep exfoliant moist:**
   - Apply cotton eye pads
   - Steam skin for 5-10 minutes

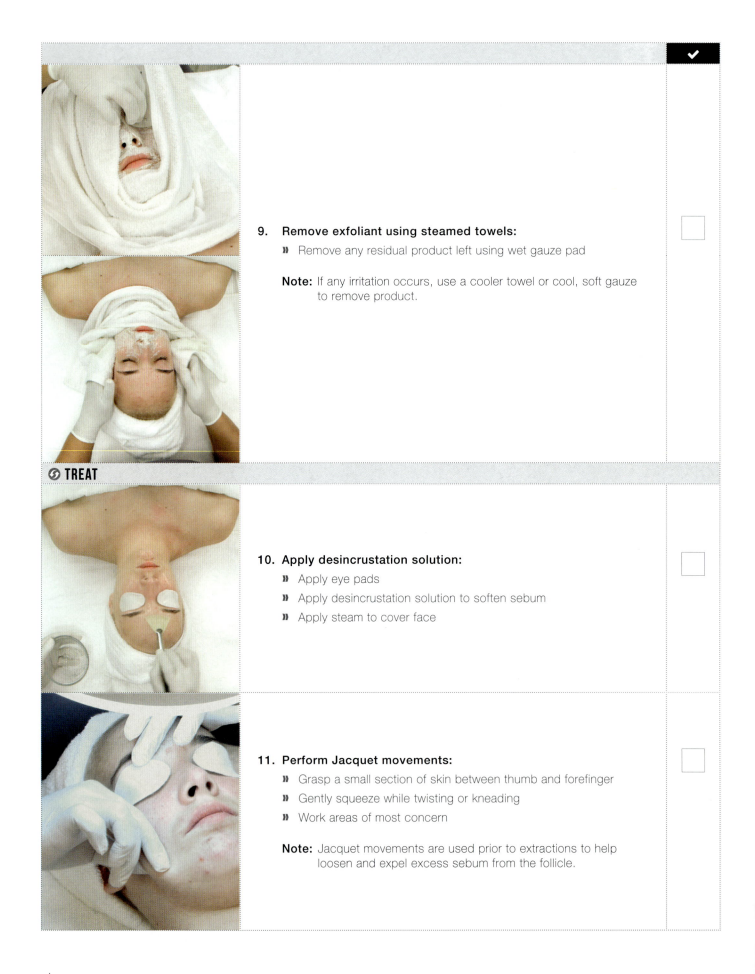

9. **Remove exfoliant using steamed towels:**
   - » Remove any residual product left using wet gauze pad

   Note: If any irritation occurs, use a cooler towel or cool, soft gauze to remove product.

TREAT

10. **Apply desincrustation solution:**
    - » Apply eye pads
    - » Apply desincrustation solution to soften sebum
    - » Apply steam to cover face

11. **Perform Jacquet movements:**
    - » Grasp a small section of skin between thumb and forefinger
    - » Gently squeeze while twisting or kneading
    - » Work areas of most concern

    Note: Jacquet movements are used prior to extractions to help loosen and expel excess sebum from the follicle.

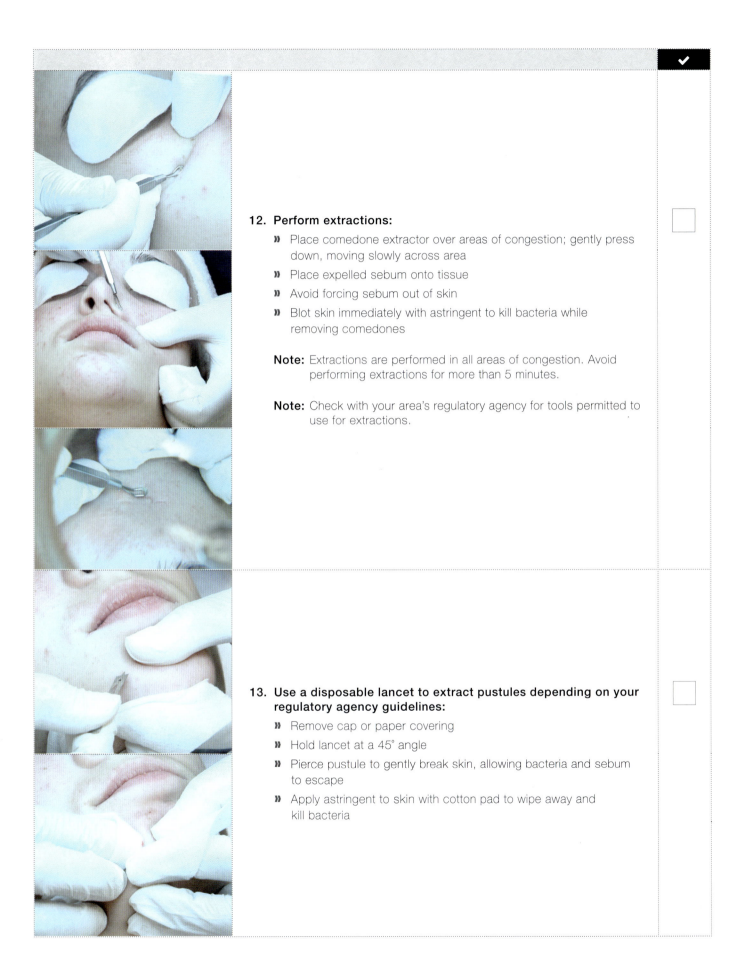

12. **Perform extractions:**
    - » Place comedone extractor over areas of congestion; gently press down, moving slowly across area
    - » Place expelled sebum onto tissue
    - » Avoid forcing sebum out of skin
    - » Blot skin immediately with astringent to kill bacteria while removing comedones

    Note: Extractions are performed in all areas of congestion. Avoid performing extractions for more than 5 minutes.

    Note: Check with your area's regulatory agency for tools permitted to use for extractions.

13. **Use a disposable lancet to extract pustules depending on your regulatory agency guidelines:**
    - » Remove cap or paper covering
    - » Hold lancet at a 45° angle
    - » Pierce pustule to gently break skin, allowing bacteria and sebum to escape
    - » Apply astringent to skin with cotton pad to wipe away and kill bacteria

TREAT

14. Dispose of lancet immediately in a sharps container after use.

15. After the extractions, blot the entire face with astringent.

    Why do you think the skin is blotted instead of wiped with astringent?

MASK

16. Apply mask to upper chest, neck and face:
    » Apply eye pads

    ◐ For this client, a soothing clay mask was chosen to calm the skin.

17. Remove steamed towels from hot-towel cabinet, allow to cool.

18. After mask has set, remove with the cool towels.

19. Apply astringent instead of a toner after mask removal.

PROTECT

20. Apply an antibacterial treatment serum to the skin using gloved hands, followed by a moisturizer designed for oily skin and a 30 SPF or higher.

Acne treatments will benefit from the use of devices such as galvanic and direct high frequency, which will be covered in the *Facial Treatment With Devices* area of study.

COMPLETION

» Complete the "Teach" phase of the Skin Assessment and Recommendation system
» Include written after-care instructions that outline specific products to use within 48 hours and lifestyle cautions such as avoid picking or exfoliating areas that have been extracted and avoid wearing makeup until the next day
» Discard single-use supplies
» Disinfect tools and multi-use supplies
» Disinfect workstation and arrange in proper order
» Place used towels in a closed container or place in washing machine
» Change treatment table linens to prepare for next client

60 minutes Commercially Accepted Time

My Speed

INSTRUCTIONS:
Record your time in comparison with the commercially accepted time. Then list here how you could improve your performance.

CHEMICAL EXFOLIATION 107ᴱ.15

EXPLORE //

Do you know how fast dead cells turn over and are replaced by new cells?

Always follow appropriate infection control guidelines according to your regulatory agency.

INSPIRE //

Clients seek out estheticians who can help reduce fine lines and wrinkles for a smooth and soft result.

ACHIEVE //

Following this lesson on *Chemical Exfoliation,* you'll be able to:

» Identify the benefits of different types of chemical exfoliation services and exfoliants

» Explain the function and infection control guidelines for chemical exfoliation products, tools, supplies and equipment

» Describe the skills related to chemical exfoliation

» State the service essentials related to chemical exfoliation

» Offer examples of chemical exfoliation care and safety guidelines

» Summarize the three areas of a chemical exfoliation service

FOCUS //

CHEMICAL EXFOLIATION

Chemical Exfoliation Service

Chemical Exfoliation Products, Tools, Supplies and Equipment

Chemical Exfoliation Skills

Chemical Exfoliation Service Essentials

Chemical Exfoliation Care and Safety Guidelines

Chemical Exfoliation Service Overview and Rubric

Chemical exfoliation, also known as a chemical peel, is the use of chemical solutions to dissolve or reduce dead skin cells and desmosomes. This promotes cell turnover and induces desquamation (shedding, peeling or coming off in scales) of the stratum corneum. This service is very popular and you will perform this treatment in most work environments.

Before performing a chemical exfoliation service, it is important to understand:

» Types of chemical exfoliation services
» Products, tools and supplies needed for treatment
» Service guidelines
» Care and safety guidelines for you and your client

In this lesson we will focus on acid peels, but remember that enzyme exfoliation is also considered a chemical exfoliation, as you learned in the *Skin Theory* lesson.

CHEMICAL EXFOLIATION SERVICE

Chemical exfoliation services are as varied as the manufacturer products. This is one service where additional training with the manufacturer of your chemical exfoliation products is advised and can be required by your regulatory agency before you work on clients.

Clients often choose a chemical exfoliation as their first service with an esthetician due to claims about quickly improving the appearance of the skin. Most treatments improve:

» Texture
» Fine lines and wrinkles
» Pigmentation
» Hydration
» Some forms of scarring

Schedule chemical exfoliation treatments in a series of 4-8 sessions. The type of chemical exfoliation determines the frequency. Schedule chemical exfoliation services every 14 days. A series of treatments every 3-4 months is the typical recommendation. Treatments can also be scheduled once a month as needed. The schedule depends on the product strength and the client's tolerance to chemical exfoliation treatments.

Chemical exfoliation and peels can result in burns that require medical attention and can scar a client. It's important to obtain as much training as possible in working with chemicals. Be sure you perform a skin assessment before applying a chemical exfoliant, follow the manufacturer's instructions and clearly explain after-care guidelines.

TYPES OF CHEMICAL EXFOLIATION

Consider different types of chemical exfoliation by looking at the depth of the peeling product, actions on the skin and the target of the acid medium. Just looking at the type of acid used is not an effective way to determine depth. Start with understanding the three depths of chemical exfoliation:

- Superficial/Light
- Medium
- Deep

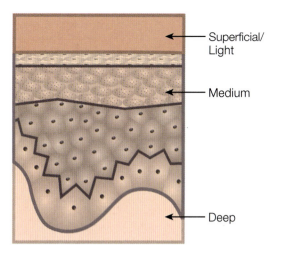

SUPERFICIAL/LIGHT

Superficial and light peels impact the skin up to 0.1 mm (.0040") of the epidermis. This level of exfoliation typically uses multiple types of acids such as glycolic acid, salicylic acid and mandelic acid. The action is dependent on the type of acid, contact time and overall formulation. Side effects such as mild peeling, redness and flakey skin are common and can last for 7-10 days. These types of peels should not be performed closer than 14 days between treatments. Safe application of these types of chemical exfoliation also depends on how well you do your skin assessment. All Fitzpatrick skin types can have this level of service if skin is prepared correctly.

MEDIUM

Medium-depth peels impact all of the epidermis into the papillary layer. They generally do not fall into a scope of practice for estheticians. These peeling agents are usually trichloroacetic acid (TCA) of 35% or greater and pyruvic acid. This level of chemical peel should be done under medical professional supervision and has a high risk of side effects if done incorrectly; some sedation may be needed. This type of peel causes your client to look unappealing for at least 10 days post-peel. Be sure to understand the healing cycle for this type of chemical peel even though you may not perform this service under your esthetics license. Services such as a hydrating facial can be extremely helpful at a certain point in the healing process.

Use caution when working with Fitzpatrick skin types 4-6. Examples of medium-depth peels are:

- TCA (Trichloroacetic acid) 35%-40%
- Pyruvic Acid 40%-60%

> **Timeline for medium-depth peels:**
> - 0-2 days: Skin appears pink and inflamed
> - 3-4 days: Skin develops dark areas where acid was applied; this can look brown-gray
> - 5-10 days: Skin starts to peel off in sheets. Redness may still be present and can continue.
> - After 10 days: Use a gentle facial treatment with a light enzyme exfoliation to help skin heal; this needs approval from the medical professional who approved the initial treatment

DEEP

Deep chemical peels affect the epidermis into the reticular dermis. This is a procedure that must be done in a physician's office and requires patient sedation. Complications are frequent so deep chemical peels are not done often due to laser resurfacing having a better outcome with less complication. The physician who performs this procedure must direct post-care. Examples of deep chemical peels include:

- Phenol
- Carbolic acid

pH SCALE

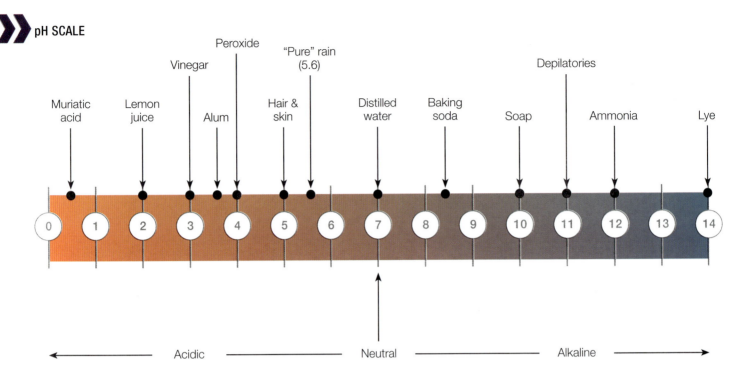

CHEMICAL EXFOLIANTS

To choose the best chemical exfoliant, it is important to understand the different types of acids, the impact of pH on effectiveness and how they work. Always follow manufacturer's instructions for client safety and predictable results.

Exfoliant acids are in three categories:
- Alpha-hydroxy acids (AHAs)
- Beta-hydroxy acids (BHAs)
- Blended or designer acids

The pH is important in peel products. As you learned in the pH lesson, acids have a pH of 1 to 6 (neutral is 7 and alkalis range from 8 to 14). pH is part of a complex equation when determining the efficacy of an acid formulation. Acid peel effectiveness is related to the pH of the solution, free-acid level and buffering of the solution. Free-acid is the active acid part of a peel. Every acid exfoliation ingredient has a free-acid number.

A formulation with a free-acid level less than the pH means its exfoliation effectiveness is less active. A lower pH can cause more irritation but does not necessarily go any deeper. The formulation, types of buffering agents and other ingredients also make a difference.

Many regulatory agencies have limited esthetician use of chemical exfoliation to a 3.0 pH to simplify a complex concept.

Key things to understand pH are:
- Lower pH is more acidic
- pH below 2.5 can cause irritation
- Lower pH can increase efficacy, depending on the acid
- The formulation determines effectiveness and depth based on buffering ingredients, free-acid amount and type, pH and how the chemical exfoliation is applied

Be guided by your regulatory agency to determine which types of acid exfoliation you can use.

ACID PERCENTAGE

The percentage of a chemical exfoliation indicates how much peeling agent the peel has. So, a 15% glycolic acid peel has less glycolic acid than a 50% glycolic acid peel. A common misconception is that if a peel has a high percentage, it means an esthetician can't use it. The total formulation is the true indicator of how effective a chemical exfoliant is.

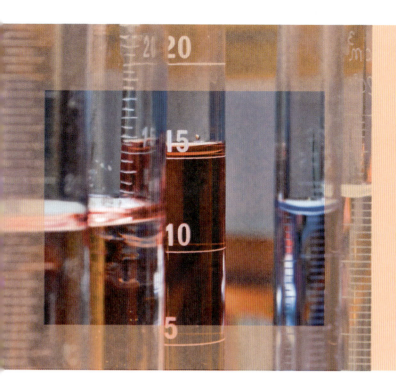

DISCOVER**MORE**

The Next Generation
A new generation of acids is poly-hydroxy acids (PHAs). Lactobionic and gluconolactone are examples of PHAs. These acids are compatible with clinically sensitive skin types, such as patients diagnosed with atopic dermatitis and rosacea. PHAs also enhance the skin barrier—an important benefit for people with compromised skin conditions. Research to learn more about this new generation of acids.

ALPHA-HYDROXY ACIDS

Alpha-hydroxy acid, or AHA, is a term for a group of acids that occur naturally in food. These include glycolic, lactic, phytic and mandelic acids. While all of these acids vary in structure, size and weight, they all have a hydroxyl group in the alpha carbon position—hence the name, alpha hydroxy. AHAs are considered water-soluble and must be neutralized before removing.

With continuous use, key benefits of AHAs are that they aid in normalizing skin functions, like achieving the proper rate of exfoliation and increased hydration. AHAs also encourage collagen deposition and fibroblast formation. AHAs penetrate the corneum via the intercellular matrix and loosen the bonds between the cells called desmosomes. The intercellular matrix between the skin cells consists of ceramides, lipids, glycoproteins, and active enzymes. AHAs also stimulate the production of intercellular lipids. Glycolic acid can penetrate into the epidermis more effectively because it has the smallest molecular size of the AHAs.

Common AHAs are:

Acids	Derived From
Glycolic	Sugar cane
Lactic	Sour milk
Citric	Citrus fruits
Phytic	Rice
Mandelic	Almonds
Tartaric	Grapes
Malic	Apples

BETA-HYDROXY ACID (SALICYLIC ACID)

Beta-hydroxy acid (BHA) is also known as salicylic acid. Salicylic acid (SA) is a unique hydroxy acid since it's lipophilic, or attracted to oil. Salicylic acid penetrates the sebaceous material in the hair follicle, causing exfoliation—even in oily areas of the face and scalp.

When you consider the use of SA in a chemical peel:

» SA has anti-inflammatory properties; ideal for treating acne and oily skin.

» SA is known as a keratolytic, meaning that proteins (dead skin cells) are dissolved when applied.

» SA is derived from sweet birch, willow bark and wintergreen. Aspirin is derived from salicylates, so clients allergic to aspirin may be allergic to salicylic ingredients.

» SA is self-neutralizing and does not require a neutralizer like AHAs do; apply quickly to avoid deactivating the formulation.

Salicylic acid is also a component of a Jessner's peel solution. Jessner's solution is a mixture of salicylic acid, resorcinol, lactic acid and ethanol, used both for superficial and medium-depth peels, depending upon the concentration of acid and layers applied. Jessner's can be considered out-of-scope in some areas. You need additional training to use Jessner's peel, such as through a manufacturer or advanced classes.

BLENDED ACIDS/DESIGNER ACIDS

Blended acids or "designer acids" are popular combinations of formulations that are specific to a manufacturer. Combinations are based on the effect that the manufacturer wants to see. Some common blends are salicylic acid with low levels of TCA (trichloroacetic acid) and skin-lightening ingredients like kojic acid.

Key things about these types of peels:

» Always follow manufacturer's instructions for use.
» Identify the benefits from your training.
» Do not blend these formulations with any other acid formulations.

> Azelaic acid is another new ingredient available to improve the effectiveness of a chemical exfoliation. It is not an AHA or BHA but can be used as a daily treatment for rosacea and acne. This ingredient comes from wheat and grains, and also from yeast your skin naturally produces. Azelaic acid has anti-inflammatory and antibacterial properties and is often included in a blended acid or designer acid peel.

BENEFITS OF CHEMICAL EXFOLIATION

Chemical exfoliation benefits the skin and is a part of an effective treatment plan.

Benefits are:

» Improved texture, barrier function and moisture retention.
» Increased cell turnover rate, hydration and intercellular lipids.
» Reduced fine lines, wrinkles and surface pigmentation.
» Smoother and softer skin.
» Improved skin conditions such as acne, hyperpigmentation, clogged pores and dry skin.
» Potentially stimulating elastin and collagen production.

Studies have found regular chemical exfoliation can help reduce abnormal skin growths such as actinic keratosis (AK). These are commonly known as pre-cancerous lesions.

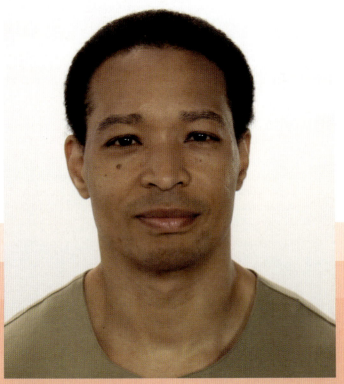
Before

After

CHEMICAL EXFOLIATION PRODUCTS, TOOLS, SUPPLIES AND EQUIPMENT

The products, tools, supplies and equipment that you need are a general guideline for chemical exfoliation. Often manufacturers will sell kits that have the products that you need chemical exfoliation procedure. It's important to understand chemicals you work with before using them on your clients.

CHEMICAL EXFOLIATION PRODUCTS

Before performing a chemical peel, you will need the following products:

PRODUCTS	FUNCTION
Occlusive Skin Protectant	Protects delicate areas around nose and eyes; an example is petroleum jelly.
Cleanser	Cleanses face; gel to de-fat (de-grease) the skin
Toner	An astringent or prep product recommended by manufacturer
Superficial Chemical Peel	Performs exfoliation action; use one version based on skin assessment AHA – Alpha-hydroxy acid » Glycolic acid » Lactic acid » Designer peel blends BHA – Beta-hydroxy acid » Salicylic acid » Designer peel blends

PRODUCTS	FUNCTION
Neutralizer	Stops action of chemical exfoliant Neutralizing gel paste or agent (usually sodium bicarbonate and water) **USE FOR EVERY AHA CHEMICAL PEEL** Not necessary for BHA peels
Mask	*Non-setting* – Gentler than setting mask; remains moist, calming and hydrating
Serum	Delivers calming and soothing ingredients
Moisturizer	Replenishes skin's moisture after peel solution is removed Use a cream designed for calming and barrier repair
Sunscreen	Protects skin from UV exposure following treatment; non-chemical only Do not use if performing service in the evening

107E.15 | CHEMICAL EXFOLIATION

CHEMICAL EXFOLIATION TOOLS

You will need a number of tools to perform superficial chemical peels:

TOOLS	FUNCTION	CLEANING GUIDELINES	DISINFECTION GUIDELINES
Peel Applicator	» Applies solution	» Single-use item, must be discarded.	» Cannot be disinfected.
Spatula	» Removes products from container; helps prevent cross-contamination » Applies masks	» If single-use item, must be discarded. » If multi-use item, preclean with soap and water. » Rinse well.	» If multiple-use item, immerse in an approved EPA-registered disinfectant solution.
Small Mixing Bowl	» Holds peel solution, cleanser, mask and moisturizer » Use multiple small bowls	» Preclean with soap and water. » Rinse well.	» Immerse in an approved EPA-registered disinfectant solution. » Rinse well. » Dry appropriately.
Eye Protection	» Protects eyes » Laser eye pads shields very effective and adheres to skin around eyes	» Single-use item; must be discarded.	» Cannot be disinfected.

CHEMICAL EXFOLIATION SUPPLIES

You will need a number of supplies to perform superficial chemical peels:

SUPPLIES	FUNCTION	CLEANING GUIDELINES	DISINFECTION GUIDELINES
4 X 4 Non-Woven Gauze Wipe	» To remove cleanser	» Single-use item, must be discarded.	» Cannot be disinfected.
Cotton Round	» Used damp to remove products from face and neck » 4" (10.16 cm) diameter for cleansing pads » 2" (5.08 cm) diameter for individual eye pads » 2" (5.08 cm) by 6" (15.2 cm)		
Single-Use Towel	» Used on supply tray to provide a clean workspace » Paper towels can be used		
Single-Use Gloves	» Protect hands		
Sheet, Blanket	» Drapes facial treatment table	» Remove hair and debris. » Wash in washing machine after each use at recommended temperature.	» Use an approved laundry additive if required by regulatory agency. » Dry thoroughly.
Headband or Hairnet	» Protects client's hair from products » Keeps client's hair out of face		

107E.15 | CHEMICAL EXFOLIATION

SUPPLIES	FUNCTION	CLEANING GUIDELINES	DISINFECTION GUIDELINES
Tissues	» Blot skin dry	» Single-use item, must be discarded.	» Cannot be disinfected.
Cotton Swab	» Applies barrier product		
Towel	» Drapes client's upper chest » Protects the hairline » As a cool towel wrap to remove products	» Remove hair and debris. » Wash in washing machine after each use at recommended temperature.	» Use an approved laundry additive if required by regulatory agency. » Dry thoroughly.
Client Gown	» Covers and allows client to remove clothing (to prevent staining)		

CHEMICAL EXFOLIATION EQUIPMENT

You will need a variety of equipment to perform superficial chemical peels:

EQUIPMENT	FUNCTION	INFECTION CONTROL AND SAFETY GUIDELINES
Magnifying Lamp	» Illuminates and amplifies skin to determine skin conditions	» Clean regularly with a soft cloth. » Disinfect at end of each day following manufacturer's instructions with disinfectant solution and allow to dry. » Be aware of the electrical cord with floor-standing model. » Remove fingerprints from lens with a cloth dampened with water. » Avoid use of alcohol or solvents on lens. » Check that bulb is secure.
Wood's Lamp	Determines: » Skin type » Pigmentation conditions	» Clean regularly with a soft cloth. » Clean at end of each day following manufacturer's instructions with disinfectant solution on handle and allow to dry. » Use caution around electrical cords. » Remove fingerprints from lens with a dampened cloth » Avoid use of alcohol or solvents on lens. » Check that bulb is secure.

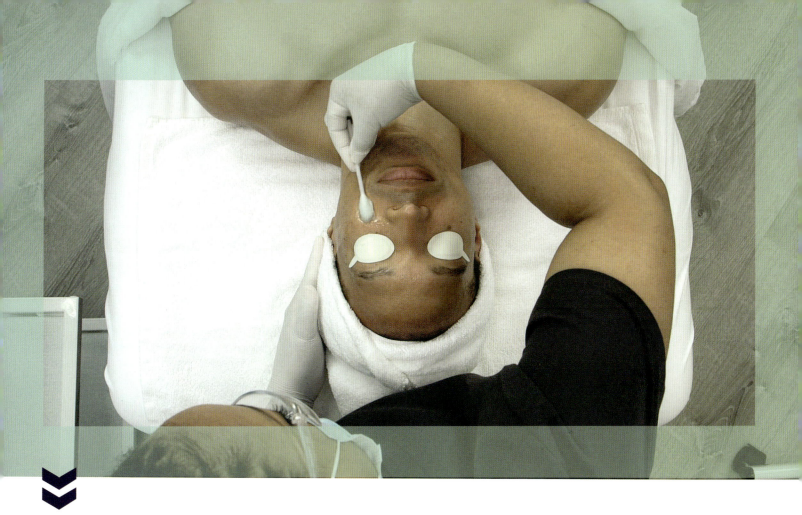

CHEMICAL EXFOLIATION SKILLS

When performing chemical peels, you should rely on proper skin assessment, application procedure and correctly neutralizing chemical exfoliation products. All of the skills you learned in the facial treatment section will apply here, except for massage.

CHEMICAL EXFOLIATION DRAPING GUIDELINES

Chemical exfoliation draping is exactly the same as a facial treatment draping with the addition of specific protection considerations. See the *Facial Treatment Skills* lesson for appropriate draping set-up.

Chemical exfoliation draping special considerations:

Eyes	» Must be covered at all times. Chemical exfoliation solution could cause burning and irritation. Ideally use laser eye shields, as they adhere to the skin. » If not available, apply a layer of occlusive skin protectant around eyes and secure with eye pads.
Hair	» Keep covered with towel; hairnets will not provide protection if chemical exfoliant drips on hair.
Nose/Lips	» Apply skin protectant around nostrils and lips.

CHEMICAL EXFOLIATION APPLICATION TECHNIQUES

The techniques you use to apply a chemical peel depend on the type of exfoliant; follow manufacturer's instructions.

In general, follow these guidelines:

Pre-Cleanse	» Use a non-oily makeup remover over eyes and face or gentle cleanser.
Analyze	» Perform the skin assessment; identify Fitzpatrick skin type for appropriate chemical solution use. » Use a Wood's lamp to identify level of oiliness and types of pigmentation present.
Cleanse	» Use a gel cleanser to de-grease the skin as well as any manufacturer-recommended prep solution. » Protect eyes, nose and lips after this step.
Exfoliant	» Work in a consistent pattern applying the correct amount of solution; be sure to cover all areas of the face and neck. » Process for the recommended time; watch for extreme redness and discomfort. » Use a handheld fan for AHAs, if needed. » DO NOT use a handheld fan for BHAs; this neutralizes the BHA too quickly.
Neutralize	» If using an AHA chemical exfoliant, apply a generous amount of recommended neutralizer. » Remove with cool wet towel. » Be sure to check in with your client about areas that may still be tingling; no tingling should be felt after this step. » If using a BHA, remove with a cool wet towel, then proceed to mask step.
Mask	» Use a generous amount of non-setting mask to cool and calm the skin. » Leave on for recommended time, usually 10 minutes. » Remove with cool wet towel.
Protect	» Use soothing serums and moisturizer that support skin barrier repair. » Avoid active ingredients. » Use a non-chemical sunscreen such as zinc oxide if service is done during the day.

Part of chemical exfoliation skills is understanding the correct post-care guidelines for a superficial chemical peel. Your manufacturer should provide specific products and directions as well. Be sure to give these directions to your clients:

Day 1-2:
» Avoid direct sun exposure
» Do not use exfoliants or active ingredients like retinol or other acids
» Keep skin moisturized as needed (re-epithelialization occurs within the first 24 hours; skin must stay hydrated)

Day 3-7:
» Use recommended home-care products
» Limit use of active serums like retinol and glycolic acid
» Use daily SPF even if not in direct sunlight

Day 7+:
» Regular home-care routine can continue with the use of active products
» Continue SPF daily

Based on the results your client desires, the next chemical exfoliation can be scheduled from day 14 on. A series of at least four superficial chemical exfoliation services is needed to see results on conditions like pigmentation and aging.

CHEMICAL EXFOLIATION SERVICE ESSENTIALS

Service essentials for chemical exfoliation should follow the same guidelines as the facial treatment with emphasis on determining which chemical exfoliation product would be best for your client as well as identifying potential contraindications and cautions.

THE FOUR SERVICE ESSENTIALS (4 Cs)

1. Connect

Establishes rapport and builds credibility with each client
- Prepare for client
- Preview client record if available
- Review client intake form for first-time clients

2. Consult

Analyzes client wants and needs, visualizes the end result, organizes the plan for follow-through and obtains client consent
- Observe and Analyze steps

3. Create

Produces functional, predictable and pleasing results
- Treat step

4. Complete

Reviews the service experience and client satisfaction, offers product recommendations, expresses appreciation and provides follow-up
- Teach step

CONNECT

Ways to communicate and build your relationship with your client are:

- Meet and greet the client with a welcoming smile and a pleasant tone of voice.
- Be friendly and communicate clearly to build rapport and develop a relationship with them.
- Preview the client record for returning clients and review the client intake form for first-time clients.
- Talk about their lifestyle and their concerns.

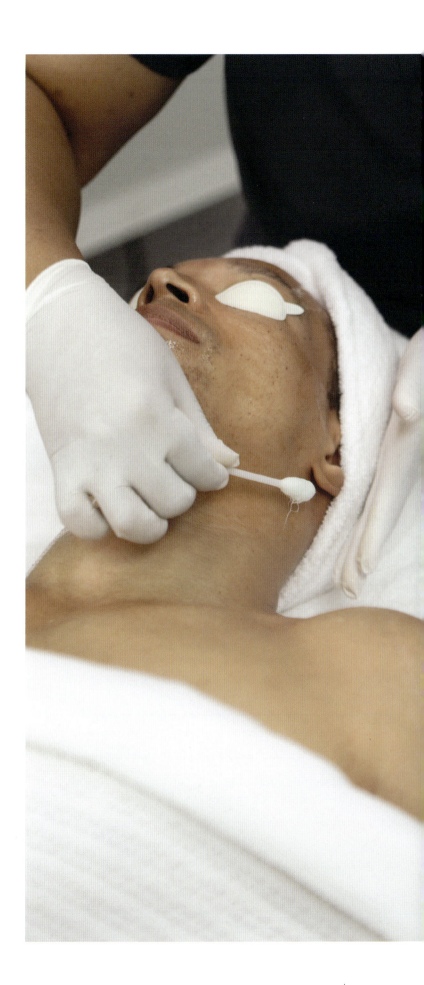

CHEMICAL EXFOLIATION

CONSULT

The consultation is crucial to the facial treatment, even for returning clients. You can discuss any concerns and ensure there are no contraindications or medical issues that could pose a problem. This part of the 4 Cs includes the Observe and Analyze steps discussed in the *Skin Assessment and Recommendation System* lesson. To learn more, see the lesson of the same name in the *Skin* area of study.

Every time a client visits, review records and comments from the last treatment and make sure there are no changes needed. Best practice is to have the client sign in agreement that there are no changes to their information.

Ask questions to discover client needs:

» Assess why the client is requesting a chemical exfoliation service.

» Explain the risks, post-care requirements and how the chemical exfoliation service will be performed.

» Gain feedback and consent from your client.

Use open questions to:
» Discover client's needs
» Encourage client to talk
» Prevent clients from answering with a simple 'Yes' or 'No'

For example:
» "Tell me about your lifestyle/activities."
» "What is your normal facial care procedure?"
» "What other treatments have you had?"

SKIN ASSESSMENT AND RECOMMENDATION SYSTEM TREATMENT PLAN

As you learned in the *Skin* area of study, there are four steps to complete within the Skin Assessment and Recommendations System: Observe, Analyze, Treat and Teach. The Consult service essential is where you perform Observe and Analyze steps. This includes:

» Review client intake form.

» Analyze client's face and complete appropriate sections of skin charting form.

» Complete your observations in the skin charting form summary. Pay close attention to possible lifestyle, medical and medication use that could impact a chemical exfoliation service.

» Fill out the appropriate section(s) of the treatment record.

The type of chemical exfoliant to use is based on your client's skin assessment. Here is a general guide:

ACIDS	CONDITION CATEGORY
AHAs	Aging, texture, pigmentation, sensitivity
BHAs	Acne, pigmentation, texture
Designer Peels	Sensitivity, acne, aging

CREATE

During the chemical exfoliation treatment, use methods that ensure client comfort. Before the treatment begins, make your client aware of each step, so they can relax during the facial.

Guidelines to ensure client comfort throughout the treatment:

- Protect client by practicing infection control procedures throughout the service.
- Consider and address each client's mobility needs, such as supporting the client's knees with a bolster; be aware of the client's body language.
- Use the most appropriate draping for the client, depending on their needs.
- Ensure all necessary products and supplies are at hand to minimize noise and avoid a disjointed treatment.
- Stay focused on delivering the treatment to the best of your ability; talking during the treatment may prove difficult and distracting.

Watch for Client's Body Language

Negative
- Looking away
- Tense shoulders
- Clenched hands
- Flinching
- Shallow breathing

Positive
- Deep or even breathing
- Relaxed body
- Open hands

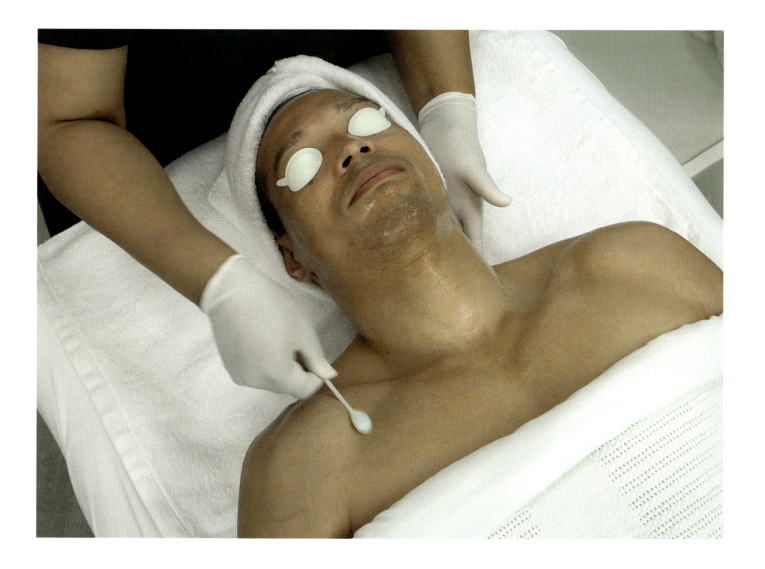

DISCOVER MORE

Working With Diverse Skin Types

You can perform chemical exfoliant services on all types of skin if you choose the correct type of exfoliant, or you do pretreatment before the first service. Identifying the correct Fitzpatrick type and making modifications is a good start. Research and discover more about the effects of various chemical exfoliants and their effects on different skin tones.

COMPLETE

Complete includes the Teach step—explaining post-care guidelines, home-care recommendations, instructions and a future treatment plan. Complete is as important as the analysis. Gathering feedback and answering questions—with your client's goals in mind—helps clarify what they need to do to get the results they want.

To solidify your relationship with your client during the Complete phase of the facial service, follow these guidelines:

» Request feedback from your client.
» Provide aftercare advice once the client is ready, and discuss with them:
  » Potential chemical exfoliation side effects and when to get help if needed
  » Post-care guidelines for superficial chemical exfoliation
  » How many treatments may be needed to see results
» Create a treatment plan with recommended time frame for re-booking the service:
  » Record recommended products on client treatment record
  » Record results of service including documenting type of superficial peel, duration left on skin and location applied
  » Invite to purchase the post-care products
» Escort your client to the reception area, encourage them to prebook for next time and ask for referrals for future services.
» Thank your client for visiting the salon/spa and leave them with a warm goodbye.
» Discard single-use items, clean and disinfect multi-use supplies.
» Change treatment table linens and prepare for next client.

Following the treatment, remember to record:

» Details of facial within the treatment record
» Recommended products/services for future visits
» Information of particular interest, such as any reactions to the treatment or client feedback
» Aftercare, with any individual notes

CHEMICAL EXFOLIATION CARE AND SAFETY GUIDELINES

When you perform a chemical exfoliation, there are some risks you need to be aware of. Contra-actions can happen when you perform an incorrect skin assessment, clients do not follow post-care instructions, or the service is performed incorrectly, such as not neutralizing an AHA.

Contra-actions you may see are:

» Chemical burns
» Itching and irritation
» Dry uncomfortable skin
» Post-inflammatory pigmentation

CHEMICAL EXFOLIATION TREATMENT ROOM GUIDELINES

General treatment room guidelines learned in facial treatments apply for chemical exfoliation services as well. For example, ventilation may need to be modified based on the type of exfoliant used.

Lighting
- Make sure it's bright enough for you to work but dark enough for a relaxing environment
- Enhance lighting by using a magnifying lamp through the whole exfoliation service

Temperature
- Balance temperature to be warm enough for the client and cool enough for you
- Keep most products, especially clay-based products, cool for good application
- Use recommended treatment room temperature at 70°-75°F (21°-24°C)
- Drape clients using the appropriate blankets

Ventilation
- Provide adequate ventilation to remove odors and moisture (humidity)
- Use an air filter to clean the air while using chemical exfoliants
- Keep air moving to ensure freshness and cleanliness

Ergonomics
- Position and organize the work cart or workstation in a convenient manner; products should be situated in order of use for smooth and efficient service
- Ensure client feels that each product is seamlessly obtained and applied without too much noise or movement
- Tuck away any loose wires on equipment safely to avoid any hazard
- Position treatment table at a height that helps you maintain good posture; however, the client must be able to easily access the treatment table, using either an adjustable treatment table or footstool

Infection Control
- Ensure all infection control procedures are followed for all clients
- Have clean client draping, headbands and towels ready

CHEMICAL EXFOLIATION TREATMENT ROOM PREPARATION AND SET-UP

Preparation for a chemical exfoliation treatment is similar to a facial treatment setup. The only differences are dispensing of chemical exfoliants before application and disposal of unused chemical exfoliants.

Treatment Table
- Drape in preparation for the client, with all the necessary towels
- Clean facial drape set out for client
- Adjust table height for easy client access

Work Cart
- Place paper or disposable towel on top of cart
- Have products arranged in order of use; be sure you can access additional items used after skin analysis
- Ensure chemical exfoliant lid is tightly closed until right before application; this is very important for BHAs as they self-neutralize within two minutes
- Ensure that all lids and dispensers are clean and work properly
- Make sure water bowl and small dispense bowls are clean and prepared
- Arrange brushes, tools and supplies in order of use
- Ensure cool towels are prepared and placed in large bowl or other container

Infection Control and Safety
- Prepare disinfection area with proper disinfectant, containers and cleanser
- Disinfection area should be free of debris
- Be sure sink is cleaned with no visible debris
- Have single-use gloves readily available
- Place trash can close to work area and cover with lid
- Discard chemical exfoliant saturated with baking soda into trash; do not place back into chemical exfoliant bottle

CHEMICAL EXFOLIATION CONTRAINDICATIONS

As you learned in the *Facial Treatment Guest Experience* lesson, contraindications refer to conditions that prevent treatment. These contraindications apply to every facial treatment including chemical exfoliation. With chemical exfoliation, when in doubt, do not perform the service as this is a high risk to your client. Treatment is prohibited on clients with the conditions below unless otherwise noted. Refer to the *Facial Treatment Guest Experience* lesson for general visual signs for each type of contraindication

CONTRAINDICATIONS	ALERT	TREATMENT DETAILS
Autoimmune Disorders » Lupus » Psoriasis	Avoid Treatment	» Avoid treatment when rash or flare-up is present » Service cannot be performed
Known Allergies » Latex Gloves » Salicylic Acid » Aspirin	Avoid Treatment	» Avoid treatment using known allergen
Active Infection » Virus » Tuberculosis » Rhinovirus (cold) » Bacteria » MRSA » HIV/AIDS » Influenzas	Avoid Treatment	» Active infections are a contraindication and service cannot be performed » Use caution with HIV/AIDS – this is not a contraindication, but standard precaution guidelines should be followed
Viral Skin Infections » Herpes Simplex (active outbreak) » Papilloma » Tinea Corporis » Herpes Zoster » Candida Albicans » Warts	Avoid Treatment	» Active infections are a contraindication and service cannot be performed
Bacterial Skin Infections » Impetigo » Blepharitis » Boils » Stye » Bacterial Conjunctivitis » Cellulitis	Avoid Treatment	» Active infections are a contraindication and service cannot be performed
Skin Cancer Growth Signs include: » Asymmetry » Color » Elevated » Border » Diameter	Avoid Treatment	» Avoid treatment on area of cancerous growth, biopsy or removal unless healed
Skin Diseases » Eczema	Avoid Treatment	» Avoid treatment if active flare-up » If no flare-up present, home care must support prescription use » Avoid high levels of active ingredients
Recent Surgery	Avoid Treatment	» Any surgery can affect the client physically » Need physician approval
Accutane (Medication)	Avoid Treatment	» Need physician approval
Vascular Disorder or Condition » Purpura » Ecchymosis	Avoid Treatment	» Service cannot be performed

CONTRAINDICATIONS	ALERT	TREATMENT DETAILS
Sebaceous Gland Disorders » Acne Grade 3 » Acne Grade 4 (nodulocystic or cystic acne) » Acne excoriée (client creates areas of scratches and open sores)	Avoid Treatment	» Medical intervention required » High level of dermal scarring possible; infection can be spread without medical intervention
Sudoriferous Gland Disorder » Miliaria Rubra » Ecchymosis	Avoid Treatment	» Service cannot be performed
Inflammation (Dermatitis) » Atopic Dermatitis » Pseudofolliculitis Barbae » Contact Dermatitis » Seborrheic Dermatitis » Pityriasis Rosea » Urticaria (Hives)	Avoid Treatment	» Service cannot be performed
Infestations » Scabies » Pediculosis	Avoid Treatment	» Service cannot be performed
Lesions (Primary and Secondary) » Plaque » Bullae » Scale » Wheal » Nodule » Fissure » Cyst » Crust » Ulcer » Vesicle » Excoriation	Avoid Treatment Use caution (avoid the area)	» Avoid treatment or use caution depending on the type of lesion
Recent Sunburn	Avoid Treatment Use caution (avoid the area)	» Avoid treatment if sunburn is on face » Use caution if sunburn is on the back or other part of body; client will be unable to lay comfortably on the treatment table
Open Sores, Excoriations, Scabbing	Avoid Treatment	» Avoid treatment and service cannot be performed » Indication of a disease process or injury » Need medical attention
Swelling, Redness	Avoid Treatment	» Avoid treatment and service cannot be performed » Indication of a disease process or injury » Need medical attention

CHEMICAL EXFOLIATION CAUTIONS

Many medical conditions are not considered a contraindication for a chemical exfoliation treatment. Instead you can make modifications that allow you to perform the service without causing harm. Here is a general guideline of modifications to make when dealing with potential cautions during a chemical exfoliation treatment.

DESCRIPTION	ALERT	DESCRIPTION/MODIFICATION
Pregnancy	⚠️ Use caution	» Be aware of the client's needs and additional concerns » Adapt the client's support to accommodate their needs » BHA and AHA chemical exfoliants may be prohibited during pregnancy » Best to get physician approval
Cancer	⚠️ Use caution	» Important to know current state of cancer (active vs. remission) and if lymph nodes have been removed » If lymph nodes are removed, do not massage the area until further training has been received » Physician approval is required to perform services on patients being actively treated; remission does not require physician approval, but adjustments may be made based on client needs. » Adjust device use, massage direction and pressure » It is important to seek more information when working with cancer patients » Avoid products with high levels of active ingredients and modalities that are highly stimulating » LED devices are safer for a client with cancer
Diabetes	⚠️ Use caution	» Can cause impaired healing; reactions are common » Effects of glycation accelerated » Modalities: Chemical/mechanical exfoliation; limit mechanical exfoliation modalities, provide post-care follow-up and clear directions to avoid healing complications
Epilepsy	⚠️ Use caution	» Bright light can be a trigger, confirm with client » Modalities: Light therapy, use of magnifying lamp
Heart Conditions/ High Blood Pressure	⚠️ Use caution	» Adjust client's position; some medications can cause additional sensitivity, heat treatments » Heart rhythms and pacemakers can be affected by electrical treatment » Modalities: Raise head when client is on treatment table, help client get off table » Modify massage, increased circulation could present a risk for clients with high blood pressure or a prior stroke
Thyroid Disease	⚠️ Use caution	» Dryness, sensitivity, discoloration are common. » Modalities: Chemical/mechanical exfoliation; focus on hydration and pigmentation suppression products during treatment; post-care follow-up and clear directions must be provided to avoid healing complications

DESCRIPTION	ALERT	DESCRIPTION/MODIFICATION
Neck/Back Pain	⚠️ Use caution	» Positioning for comfort and stability is essential » Modalities: Help client get on and off the treatment table, use bolsters and heated table pad
Eye Disorders	⚠️ Use caution	» Eye disorders and allergies can cause extreme eye sensitivity » Modalities: All; cover eyes completely with appropriate eye pads, use eye cream designed for sensitivity
Autoimmune Diseases & Disorders	⚠️ Use caution	» Flares can cause increased sensitivity » Lupus – No treatment when butterfly rash is present » Modalities: Position for comfort; help client get on and off treatment table
Chronic Pain	⚠️ Use caution	» Sensitivity to touch and light, general chronic stress » Modalities: All, position for comfort, help client get on and off treatment table, use heated table pad, watch massage pressure » May be very sensitive to chemical exfoliants; check your client's comfort often
Allergies	⚠️ Use caution	» Verify with client types of triggers or ingredients that cause reactions » Avoid ingredients that cause reaction; do not use latex gloves
Sensitive, Redness-Prone Skin	⚠️ Use caution	» Redness could intensify; avoid heat, harsh scrubs, stimulating massage, mechanical treatment » Mild AHAs may be used, test before use

Cosmetic Injections	⚠️ Use caution	» Cosmetic injections require a specific waiting period before treatment:
		  » Neuromodulators – Paralyze the muscles; include Botox, Dysport and Xeomin; 48 hours
		  » Fillers: 2 weeks

Hair Removal (Waxing/Electrolysis/Laser)	⚠️ Use caution	» No chemical exfoliation 48 hours after hair removal
Chemical Peels (1 month)	⚠️ Use caution	» Medium-depth chemical peel: 1 month before superficial chemical peel can be performed
Laser Treatment (1 month)	⚠️ Use caution	» Laser resurfacing requires 1 month before any chemical exfoliation is performed

CHEMICAL EXFOLIATION

Side effects from medications vary based on the individual. Here are some general guidelines for modifications. Be sure to rely on what you see on the skin and what the disclosed medical concerns are first.

MEDICATIONS	EFFECT ON SKIN/ MODIFICATIONS
Diabetes medications	» Potential rashes and itching, treat as sensitive skin » Use a mild chemical exfoliant
Thyroid medications	» Potential thinning skin, dryness, heat sensitivity » Use chemical exfoliants like lactic acid to increase hydration
Antidepressants	» Potential photosensitivity, rash, bruising » Require high SPF daily after performing chemical exfoliation
Heart/Blood Pressure medications	» Photosensitivity, skin rash » Require high SPF daily after performing chemical exfoliation
Pain medications	» Potential allergic reaction: hives, itching, rash
Acne medications (includes Retin-A and Accutane)	» Can cause skin to blister or peel; avoid chemical exfoliation
Antibiotics	» Photosensitivity, sensitive skin
Blood Thinners	» May cause bleeding or bruising; require physician's permission for chemical exfoliation treatments
Corticosteroids	» Can cause thinning of the skin that leads to blistering or injury; avoid chemical exfoliation treatments
Sleep medications	» Potential "pins and needles" feeling in hands, arms and legs; rash

CHEMICAL EXFOLIATION CONCERNS

Chemical exfoliation concerns relate to areas that you may need additional training in or potential contra-actions that can happen while you are performing the treatment.

CONCERNS OR CONTRA-ACTIONS	WHAT TO DO
Fitzpatrick Skin Types 4-6	» Pre-treat the skin with at-home pigmentation suppressant products and mild acid exfoliation » Have client discontinue use at least 48 hours before treatment » Start low and slow, use a gentle chemical exfoliant like lactic acid, then work up to stronger formulations as you see how the skin reacts
Tattoos or Permanent Makeup	» If inflamed or recently performed service, avoid area. » Services such as a light chemical exfoliation can be done to brighten tattoos on the body when they are healed.
Piercings	» Have client remove piercing (jewelry or piece) if possible » Avoid area of piercing when applying chemical exfoliants » Protect with occlusive protectant if possible (Vaseline)
Severe Erythema **Severe Inflammation** **Rashes** (including Temporary Pustules and Papules) **Temporary Swelling**	» Discontinue treatment » Apply neutralizer » Apply cold/cool towel » Remove products and apply soothing serum
Allergic Reaction (Face and eye products) **Extreme Sensitivity or a Burning Sensation**	» Remove product and apply a cold compress » If product entered eye, use an eye bath to flush the eye » Contact medical assistance if severe » Record information on treatment record
Cancer Requires additional training	» Avoid chemical exfoliants until cleared by medical professional
Disability	» Verify type of disability and what adjustment your client needs » Check in with your client often about their comfort » Do not be afraid to ask detailed questions that pertain to their comfort » Avoid pressing for answers if client does not want to discuss » Provide proper body positioning and support with bolsters » Utilize a treatment table that is adjustable for client to access » Consider your disabled client's needs and be sure cabinets, dressers, lockers and treatment tables are adjusted to appropriate heights and position so clients can easily access them with or without assistance » Follow all regulatory laws, such as ADA (Americans With Disabilities Act) for your area » Workplace needs to be able to accommodate any equipment, such as a wheelchair, with ease

CHEMICAL EXFOLIATION ALLERGIC REACTION

An allergic reaction to chemical exfoliation can happen during or after a treatment. It is important to recognize the signs and educate your client about what to do if they get a reaction. Intense and/or widespread reactions or those that affect the client's breathing should be referred for medical help immediately.

SIGNS AND SYMPTOMS	CORRECTIVE ACTION
Urticaria (Hives)	» If in treatment – Apply neutralizer, then cool compress » Recommend antihistamine and refer directly to a physician » Call 911 if breathing is impacted
Itching	» If in treatment – Apply neutralizer, then cool compress » Recommend antihistamine, refer directly to a physician if itching gets worse within two hours » Call 911 if breathing is impacted
Erythema	» Recommend cool compress applied hourly until severe redness subsides, if not resolved within 24 hours, refer to a physician

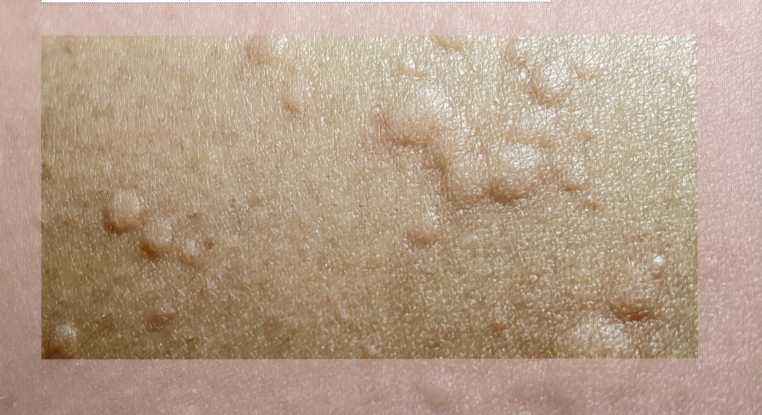

CHEMICAL EXFOLIATION CARE AND SAFETY CHART

Follow care and safety guidelines before and during the chemical exfoliation treatment:

» Ensure your safety and that of your client
» Prevent contamination and cross-contamination
» Contribute to the salon/spa care

PERSONAL CARE	CLIENT CARE PRIOR TO THE SERVICE	CLIENT CARE DURING THE SERVICE	SALON/SPA CARE
Check that your personal standards of hygiene minimize the spread of infection.	Have client put on gown or wrap-around. Drape client using appropriate draping: cocoon wrap or layered method.	Use eye pads to protect throughout the chemical exfoliation service. Protect sensitive areas such as sides of nose with occlusive protectant.	Follow health and safety guidelines, including cleaning and disinfecting procedures.
Wash hands and dry thoroughly with a single-use towel.	Use clean linens with each new client.	Be aware of skin sensitivity or cautions; check comfort level often.	Ensure equipment, including the treatment table, sink, table and counter areas are clean and disinfected before and after every service.
Disinfect workstation.	Perform correct skin assessment and identify contraindications.	Work carefully around nonremovable jewelry/piercings.	Promote a professional image by assuring your workstation is clean and organized throughout the service.
Clean and disinfect tools appropriately.	Keep lids clean and tightly closed on product jars to avoid spillage and contamination.	Be aware of nonverbal cues the client may be conveying.	Keep tools dry to avoid a short circuit when using electrical equipment.
Wear single-use gloves and additional PPE if required.	Review client intake form. Complete skin charting form, treatment record and treatment plan.	Remove all products from jars with a clean spatula.	Keep labels on all containers and store products in a cool place to protect shelf-life.
Refer to your area's regulatory agency guidelines for proper mixing/handling of disinfectant solution.		If any tools or multi-use supplies are dropped, be sure to pick them up, then clean and disinfect.	Clean/mop water spillage from floor to avoid accidental falls.
Minimize fatigue by maintaining good posture during the services.		Store soiled towels in dry, covered receptacle until laundered.	Dispose of unused chemical exfoliant by saturating with baking soda then placing in trash.

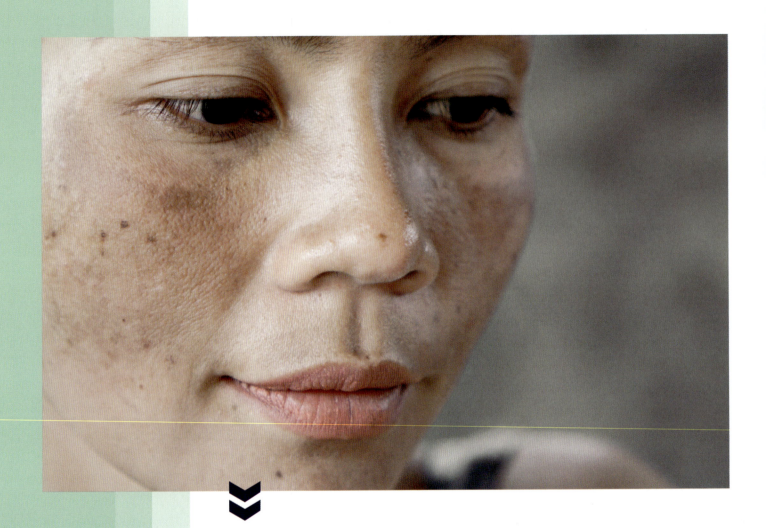

INDUSTRY CONNECTION

Some chemical peels are used in conjunction or blended with lightening agents such as hydroquinone or kojic acid.

Hydroquinone is a depigmenting agent that lightens hyperpigmentation in the skin by decreasing the number of melanocytes, which produces melanin. Hyperpigmentation happens because of increased melanocyte production, due to various considerations such as sun exposure and hormones. The ability to control this production, your skin will become more evenly toned overtime.

Kojic acid is another alternative that can be included in chemical peels. Kojic acid is a chemical produced from different types of fungi. It is also a fermented by product of rice wine and soy sauce. Like hydroquinone, it is a depigmenting agent that helps to control the melanocytes from producing excess melanin.

Both ingredients, in skin care formulations including chemical peels, are used in appropriate percentages that are safe for skin application.

CHEMICAL EXFOLIATION SERVICE OVERVIEW AND RUBRIC

The Chemical Exfoliation Service Overview identifies the three areas of all facial treatment services:

1. Preparation	Preparation provides a brief overview of the steps to follow *before* you begin a facial treatment.
2. Procedure	Procedure provides an overview of the steps that you will use *during* a facial treatment to ensure predictable results.
3. Completion	Completion provides an overview of the steps to follow *after* performing a facial treatment to ensure guest satisfaction.

A performance (assessment) rubric is a document that identifies defined criteria where levels of performance can be measured objectively. After the overview is an example of a rubric that your instructor might choose to use for scoring. The rubric is divided into three main areas—Preparation, Procedure and Completion. Each area is further divided into step-by-step procedures that will ensure client safety and satisfaction.

CHEMICAL EXFOLIATION OVERVIEW

CHEMICAL EXFOLIATION PREPARATION	» Wash hands; and set up cleansed and disinfected workstation. » Arrange disinfected tools, supplies, products; plug in devices and test; dispense gloves. » Set up treatment table; drape table; place gown on table. » Perform Observe step in Skin Assessment Recommendation System.

CHEMICAL EXFOLIATION PROCEDURE	» Drape and cover client appropriately.
	» Apply hand sanitizer and gloves.
	» Pre-Cleanse
	  » Remove makeup.
	  » Perform superficial cleanse.
	» Analyze
	  » Apply eye pads suitable for chemical exfoliation.
	  » Identify Fitzpatrick skin type and skin conditions using magnifying and Wood's lamp.
	  » Complete summary analysis.
	» Cleanse
	  » Apply de-greasing product or astringent evenly over upper chest, neck and face.
	  » Use sweeping movements using gauze pad.
	  » Blot skin dry with tissue.
	» Exfoliate
	  » Apply occlusive skin protectant to sides of nose, inner corner of eyes and lips and any minor lesions you wish to avoid.
	  » Apply chemical exfoliant product using a peel applicator onto 6 zones:
	    › Zone 1 – Forehead
	    › Zone 2 – Left cheek
	    › Zone 3 – Right cheek
	    › Zone 4 – Middle of face
	    › Zone 5 – Jawline
	    › Zone 6 – Neck and upper chest
	  » Process peel following manufacturer's instructions; use neutralizer, if applicable for the product used.
	  » Remove chemical exfoliant with a cool, damp towel in the same order peel was applied or spot areas that need it immediately.
	  » Remove chemical exfoliant eye pads
	» Mask
	  » Apply soothing non-setting mask then cotton eye pads.
	  » Allow mask to set according to manufacturer's instructions.
	  » Remove with two cool towel wraps.
	  » Apply pH-balanced toner to skin using saturated gauze pad.
	» Protect
	  » Apply eye cream.
	  » Apply calming serum, moisturizer and sun protection.

CHEMICAL EXFOLIATION COMPLETION	» Assist client in sitting up. » Complete the Teach phase of the Skin Assessment and Recommendation System. » Include written after-care instructions that outline specific products to use within 48 hours and lifestyle cautions, such as avoiding heat and sun exposure. » Discard single-use supplies. » Disinfect tools and multi-use supplies. » Disinfect workstation and arrange in proper order. » Place used towels in a closed container or place in washing machine. » Change treatment table linens to prepare for next client.

CHEMICAL EXFOLIATION RUBRIC

Allotted Time: 60 Minutes

Student Name: _____ ID Number: _____

Instructor: _____ Date: _____ Start Time: _____ End Time: _____

CHEMICAL EXFOLIATION (Live Model) – Each scoring item is marked with either a "Yes" or "No". Each "Yes" counts for one point. Total number of points attainable is 32.

CRITERIA	YES	NO	INSTRUCTOR ASSESSMENT
PREPARATION: *Did student…*			
1. Wash their hands?	☐	☐	
2. Set up workstation with properly labeled supplies?	☐	☐	
3. Place disinfected tools and supplies at a visibly clean workstation?	☐	☐	
4. Properly drape treatment table?	☐	☐	
5. Apply appropriate PPE?	☐	☐	
Connect: *Did student…*			
6. Meet and greet client with a welcoming smile and pleasant tone of voice?	☐	☐	
7. Communicate to build rapport and develop a relationship with client?	☐	☐	
Consult: *Did student…*			
8. Ask questions to discover client's wants and needs?	☐	☐	
9. Gain feedback and consent from client before proceeding?	☐	☐	
PROCEDURE: *Did student…*			
10. Properly drape client and prepare for service?	☐	☐	
11. Apply hand sanitizer and gloves if required?	☐	☐	
Create: *Did student…*			
12. Perform pre-cleanse step using appropriate makeup remover procedure?	☐	☐	
13. Perform pre-cleanse step using appropriate superficial cleanse procedure?	☐	☐	
14. Analyze client's skin using appropriate procedures and record any possible contraindications to service?	☐	☐	
15. Cleanse client's skin thoroughly using the appropriate de-greasing products, and application and removal procedures?	☐	☐	
16. Protect sides of nose, inner corners of eyes and lips and any minor lesions they wish to avoid using appropriate products and procedures?	☐	☐	
17. Obtain and apply chemical exfoliant using appropriate tools and procedures?	☐	☐	
18. Process chemical exfoliant according to manufacturer's instructions?	☐	☐	
19. Neutralize and remove chemical exfoliant using appropriate products and procedures? Spot-neutralize areas where ready prior to complete removal?	☐	☐	
20. Apply mask to calm skin using appropriate product, eye pads and application procedures?	☐	☐	
21. Remove mask using appropriate removal techniques?	☐	☐	
22. Apply toner to skin using appropriate products and procedures?	☐	☐	
23. Apply the appropriate products and procedures to moisturize and protect the skin?	☐	☐	
COMPLETION *(Complete): Did student…*			
24. Ask questions and look for verbal and nonverbal cues to determine client's level of satisfaction?	☐	☐	
25. Make professional product recommendations?	☐	☐	
26. Ask client to make a future appointment?	☐	☐	
27. End guest's visit with a warm and personal goodbye?	☐	☐	
28. Discard single-use supplies?	☐	☐	
29. Disinfect tools, multi-use supplies and equipment and arrange in proper order?	☐	☐	
30. Complete service within scheduled time?	☐	☐	
31. Complete client record?	☐	☐	
32. Wash their hands following the service?	☐	☐	

Comments: _____   TOTAL POINTS = _____ ÷ 32 = _____ %

CLIENT INTAKE FORM

Last Name: _____ First Name: _____ Date: __/__/____

Email: _____ Phone: (____) ____–_____ Birthday: __/__/____

Address: _____

City/State: _____ Zip: _____ Occupation: _____

Climate _____ Sex: ☐ Female ☐ Male

How did you hear about us? _____ Referral: _____

What skin improvements would you like to see? _____

Women: Are you pregnant or lactating? ☐ Yes ☐ No   Men: Do you experience irritation from shaving? ☐ Yes ☐ No

HEALTH HISTORY

Cancer (skin or other)	☐ Yes ☐ No	Infection (virus, bacteria)	☐ Yes ☐ No
Diabetes	☐ Yes ☐ No	HIV/AIDS	☐ Yes ☐ No
Autoimmune Disease (Lupus, RA, MS etc.)	☐ Yes ☐ No	Eye Disorders	☐ Yes ☐ No
Thyroid Disease	☐ Yes ☐ No	Chronic Pain (fibromyalgia, migraine etc.)	☐ Yes ☐ No
Neck/Back Pain	☐ Yes ☐ No	Epilepsy	☐ Yes ☐ No
Heart Problems/Blood Pressure	☐ Yes ☐ No	Hormone Issues (PCOS, Endometriosis, menopause)	☐ Yes ☐ No
Allergies (please list)	☐ Yes ☐ No	_____	

Explanation/further details: _____

SKIN HISTORY

Recent surgery (general) the last 6 months?	☐ Yes ☐ No	Laser treatments/IPL within the last month?	☐ Yes ☐ No
Recent surgery (cosmetic) the last 6 months?	☐ Yes ☐ No	Chemical peels within the last month?	☐ Yes ☐ No
Recent cosmetic injections (Botox, filler etc.)?	☐ Yes ☐ No	Loss of skin sensation?	☐ Yes ☐ No
Recent hair removal? (waxing, laser electrolysis)	☐ Yes ☐ No	Recent sunburn?	☐ Yes ☐ No
Are you under a doctor's care for skin issues?	☐ Yes ☐ No		

DAILY MEDICATIONS

☐ Accutane	☐ Retin-A	☐ Diabetes	☐ Thyroid
☐ Antibiotic	☐ Anti-Depressant	☐ Heart/Blood Pressure	☐ Corticosteroid
☐ Sleep/Anxiety	☐ Pain/NSAIDs	☐ Blood Thinner	☐ Anti-Androgen
☐ Hormones	☐ Skin Disease	☐ Other: _____	

DAILY SKIN CARE (1x, 2x, weekly, varies)

☐ Cleanser/Toner	Frequency _____	☐ Moisturizer	Frequency _____
☐ Exfoliant/Scrub	Frequency _____	☐ SPF	Frequency _____
☐ Serum/Oil	Frequency _____	☐ Night Cream	Frequency _____
☐ Mask	Frequency _____	☐ Prescription	Frequency _____
☐ Eye Cream	Frequency _____	☐ Neck Cream	Frequency _____

Reasons for use (i.e. improves wrinkles etc.): _____

CLIENT INTAKE FORM (Cont'd)
LIFESTYLE

Do you sleep from 6-8 hours a night?	☐ Yes ☐ No	If no, how many hours? _____
Do you smoke?	☐ Yes ☐ No	Cigarettes or other: _____
Do you have chronic stress?	☐ Yes ☐ No	What is your level? ☐ Low ☐ Medium ☐ High
Do you exercise regularly?	☐ Yes ☐ No	☐ Cardio ☐ Weights ☐ Yoga ☐ Other: _____
Do you use hormone replacement therapy?	☐ Yes ☐ No	
Do you get daily UV exposure?	☐ Yes ☐ No	☐ 8+ hours ☐ Less than 5 hours ☐ Less than 1 hour
Do you drink more than 7 drinks a week of alcohol?	☐ Yes ☐ No	
Do you eat at least 3 servings of vegetables a day?	☐ Yes ☐ No	
Is your intake of sugar more than 100 cals a day?	☐ Yes ☐ No	(Examples: soda, desserts, other processed foods)
Do you drink more than 2 cups a day of caffeine?	☐ Yes ☐ No	
Do you drink 8-10 glasses of water a day?	☐ Yes ☐ No	
Do you take probiotics daily?	☐ Yes ☐ No	
Do you take vitamin D3 daily?	☐ Yes ☐ No	
Do you take a multivitamin daily or omega oils?	☐ Yes ☐ No	

Future Appointments/Contact:

May I call you at your phone number to confirm future appointments?	☐ Yes ☐ No
May I text you to confirm?	☐ Yes ☐ No
May I contact you via mail/email about future promotions and news?	☐ Yes ☐ No

Service Consent:

I understand, have read and completed this questionnaire truthfully. I agree that this constitutes full disclosure, and that it supersedes any previous verbal or written disclosures. I understand that withholding information or providing misinformation may result in contraindications and/or irritation to the skin from treatments received. I understand the appointment cancellation policy. The treatments I receive here are voluntary, and I release this institution and/or skin care professional from liability and assume full responsibility thereof.

Client Signature: _____ Date: _____

SKIN CHARTING FORM

Last Name: _____ First Name: _____ Date: ___/___/_____

Client age range: ☐ 16-24 ☐ 25-40 ☐ 41-50 ☐ 51-60 ☐ 61-70+   ☐ Male: Shaving irritation? ☐   ☐ Female: Pregnant/Lactating? ☐

Reviewed client health history form? ☐ Yes ☐ No   Client daily skin care regimen verified? ☐ Yes ☐ No

Client skin history verified? ☐ Yes ☐ No   Client lifestyle factors verified? ☐ Yes ☐ No

CLIENT SKIN CARE CONCERNS (Check all that apply)

☐ Breakouts   ☐ Blackheads   ☐ Milia   ☐ Dark Circles
☐ Redness   ☐ Pigmentation   ☐ Sagging Skin   ☐ Wrinkles
☐ Rough Texture   ☐ Dryness   ☐ Dehydration   ☐ Irritation
☐ Uneven Color   ☐ Other: _____

CONTRAINDICATIONS
HEALTH

Active Cancer (in treatment) ☐ Yes ☐ No   Active Infection ☐ Yes ☐ No   Diabetes ☐ Yes ☐ No

Ingredient Allergies ☐ Yes ☐ No List: _____   Latex Allergy ☐ Yes ☐ No

☐ Other: _____

MEDICATIONS

Accutane ☐ Yes ☐ No   Skin Disease ☐ Yes ☐ No

☐ Other: _____

SKIN HISTORY

Open Lesions ☐ Yes ☐ No   Sunburn ☐ Yes ☐ No   Recent Surgery ☐ Yes ☐ No

CAUTIONS/HEALTH HISTORY FACTORS

List cautions: _____

List health history factors: _____

ANALYSIS – SKIN TYPE

Location	Description	Results	Fitzpatrick Skin Type (UV Response)	
Zones _____ _____	☐ **Pore Size:** Small pore size ☐ **Skin Thickness:** Thick skin with good elasticity, usually young clients ☐ **Wood's lamp:** Shows even blue/purple fluorescence throughout face	**Normal** Balanced oil production	☐ Type 1 (I)	Highly sensitive, always burns, never tans.
			☐ Type 2 (II)	Very sun sensitive, burns easily, tans minimally.
Zones _____ _____	☐ **Pore Size:** Small pore size ☐ **Skin Thickness:** Possible thin skin ☐ **Wood's lamp:** Shows small orange dots on nose and chin	**Dry** Limited oil production	☐ Type 3 (III)	Sun sensitive, sometimes burns, slowly tans to light brown.
Zones _____ _____	☐ **Pore Size:** Mix of medium/large pores through forehead, nose ☐ **Skin Thickness:** Thick on cheeks, thin around eyes, forehead ☐ **Wood's lamp:** Shows small orange dots through t-zone	**Combination** Uneven oil production	☐ Type 4 (IV)	Minimally sun sensitive, burns minimally, always tans to moderate brown.
Zones _____ _____	☐ **Pore Size:** Medium to large pores throughout face ☐ **Skin Thickness:** Generally thick ☐ **Wood's lamp:** Shows small orange dots throughout face and hairline, always feel oil in skin	**Oily** Widespread oil production	☐ Type 5 (V)	Sun insensitive, rarely burns, tans well.
			☐ Type 6 (VI)	Sun insensitive, rarely burns, tans well.

SKIN CHARTING FORM (Cont'd)

Last Name: _____ First Name: _____ Date: ___ / ___ / _____

ANALYSIS (LOOK/TOUCH/ASK)

Location	Look		Touch/Ask	Results
Zones: _____ _____	Color: ☐ Inflammation/ Redness (erythema) ☐ Flushed appearance (microcirculation)	Structure: ☐ Broken capillaries (telangiectasia) ☐ Edema (swelling)	☐ Do you get irritated when touched or certain products are used? ☐ Have you been diagnosed with rosacea?	Sensitivity: ☐ Rosacea ☐ Sensitive skin ☐ Allergies
Zones: _____ _____	Color: ☐ Dull appearance (gray/yellow)	Structure: ☐ Flakiness, Roughness ☐ Comedones, Milia ☐ Pustules, Papules	☐ Use dehydration test ☐ Congestion felt below skin, rough texture ☐ Does it feel like your moisturizer never penetrates? ☐ How often are you breaking out?	Texture: ☐ Acne grades 1-2 ☐ Congested skin ☐ Dehydration
Zones: _____ _____	Color: ☐ Dull appearance ☐ Discoloration ☐ Increased redness	Structure: ☐ Loose skin (elastosis) ☐ Wrinkles (superficial to deep) ☐ Folds of skin at ears ☐ Slack muscles	☐ Use elasticity test ☐ Do you feel loose skin along your jawline?	Aging: ☐ Wrinkles (fine to deep) ☐ Sagging skin ☐ Slack muscles ☐ Dull appearance ☐ Broken Capillaries
Zones: _____ _____	Color: ☐ Discolored areas on skin ☐ Loss of color in areas, ☐ Post inflammatory pigmentation (red/ brown spots)	Structure: ☐ Raised rough areas	☐ Feel pigmented areas for raised lesions ☐ Have you been diagnosed with melasma? ☐ How long after receiving an injury to your skin does the discoloration last	Pigmentation: ☐ Hyperpigmentation ☐ Melasma ☐ Hypopigmentation ☐ UV Damage
Zones: _____ _____	Color: ☐ Redness in areas of breakout (red/ brown spots)	Structure: ☐ Comedones, Milia, Pustules, Papules	☐ Raised bumps on skin ☐ Congestion felt below skin ☐ How often are you breaking out? ☐ Have you been diagnosed with acne?	Acne: ☐ Acne grades 1-2 ☐ Congested skin

SUMMARY ANALYSIS (Note pore size and location on face chart)

SKIN TYPE:
☐ Normal ☐ Oily ☐ Combination ☐ Dry

Fitzpatrick Skin Type:
☐ 1 (I) ☐ 2 (II) ☐ 3 (III) ☐ 4 (IV) ☐ 5 (V) ☐ 6 (VI)

Fitzpatrick Type Caution: _____

SKIN CONDITION: Note 2 categories and location on face chart

Sensitivity	Texture	Aging	Pigmentation
☐ Rosacea	☐ Acne grades 1-2	☐ Wrinkles (fine to deep)	☐ Hyperpigmentation
☐ Sensitive skin	☐ Congested skin	☐ Sagging skin	☐ Melasma
☐ Allergies	☐ Dehydration	☐ Slack muscles	☐ Hypopigmentation
		☐ Dull appearance	☐ UV Damage
		☐ Broken Capillaries	

LIFESTYLE/HEALTH FACTORS:

Contraindications:	_____
Cautions:	_____
Diet:	☐ Caffeine ☐ Processed Food ☐ Sugar ☐ Supplements
Sleep:	_____ Hours _____ ☐ Less than 6 hours
Stress level:	☐ Low ☐ Medium ☐ High
Climate:	☐ Hot Humid ☐ Mild Humid ☐ Cold Humid ☐ Dry ☐ Cold Dry
Exercise:	☐ Cardio ☐ Weights ☐ Yoga ☐ Other: _____
	☐ 8+ hours ☐ 4-7 hours ☐ Less than 4 hours
Smoking/Alcohol:	☐ Smoking ☐ Alcohol: More than 7 drinks a week

Notes: _____

107E.15 | CHEMICAL EXFOLIATION

TREATMENT RECORD

Esthetician initials: _____

Last Name: _____ First Name: _____ Date: ___ / ___ / _____

TREATMENTS

Treatment Chosen: _____ Modifications: _____

Expected Results: _____

Skin Changes: _____

Follow-up Date: ___ / ___ / _____

Feedback: _____

SERVICE GOALS: Choose up to 2, indicate treatment focus as it relates to INCREASE, BALANCE or DECREASE Phases

☐ Sensitivity: _____
☐ Texture: _____
☐ Aging: _____
☐ Pigmentation TR: _____
☐ Acne: _____
☐ Other: _____

PRODUCTS: Select type then list product(s)

☐ Cleansers: _____ ☐ Massage Medium: _____
☐ Toner: _____ ☐ Masks: _____
☐ Treatments/Serums: _____ ☐ Moisturizers: _____
☐ Exfoliator: _____ ☐ Other: _____

SKIN WARMING

☐ Steamer ☐ Hot Towels ☐ Occlusion ☐ Device
☐ Other: _____

MASSAGE

☐ Effleurage ☐ Petrissage ☐ Tapotement ☐ Friction/Vibration

DEVICES

☐ Galvanic Current ☐ High Frequency ☐ Microdermabrasion ☐ LED

EXTRACTION

☐ Finger Technique ☐ Comedone Extractor ☐ Cotton swabs ☐ Lancets (if allowed)

NOTES

_____

_____

_____

_____

TREATMENT PLAN

Last Name: _____ First Name: _____ Date: ___/___/_____

RECOMMENDED TREATMENTS (3-month Plan)

TREATMENT	GOAL	COSTS	FREQUENCY / NEXT APPT
_____	_____	_____	_____
_____	_____	_____	_____
_____	_____	_____	_____
_____	_____	_____	_____
_____	_____	_____	_____
_____	_____	_____	_____

RECOMMENDED HOME CARE

AM	RECOMMENDED	CURRENT USE	PM	RECOMMENDED	CURRENT USE
Cleanse:	_____	_____	Cleanse:	_____	_____
Tone:	_____	_____	Tone:	_____	_____
Treat:	_____	_____	Treat:	_____	_____
Moisture:	_____	_____	Moisture:	_____	_____
Eye Cream:	_____	_____	Eye Cream:	_____	_____
Lip Treatment:	_____	_____	Lip Treatment:	_____	_____
SPF:	_____	_____	Neck Cream:	_____	_____

Weekly Treatment

	RECOMMENDED	CURRENT USE
Exfoliation:	_____	_____
Mask:	_____	_____

INSTRUCTIONS:

_____

_____

_____

_____

CHEMICAL EXFOLIATION

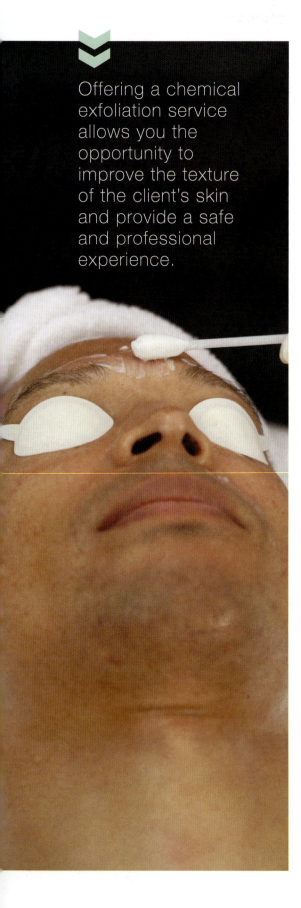

Offering a chemical exfoliation service allows you the opportunity to improve the texture of the client's skin and provide a safe and professional experience.

LESSONS LEARNED

» Chemical exfoliation is the use of chemical solutions to:
  » Exfoliate the surface of the skin
  » Promote cell turnover and induce desquamation (shedding, peeling or coming off in scales) of the stratum corneum

» The three depths of chemical exfoliants are:
  » Superficial/light
  » Medium
  » Deep

» The three types of chemical exfoliants are:
  » Alpha-hydroxy acids (AHAs)
  » Beta-hydroxy acids (BHAs)
  » Blended or designer acids

» The skills that are needed when performing chemical peels rely on proper skin assessment, application procedure and correctly neutralizing chemical exfoliation products.

» The service essentials related to chemical exfoliation are:
  » Connect – Establishes rapport and builds credibility with each client
  » Consult – Analyzes client needs, complete skin evaluation and obtain client consent
  » Create – Analyzes the client's wants and needs, establishes the client's objectives for the treatment, agrees on a treatment plan and obtains client consent
  » Complete – Reviews the service experience and client satisfaction, offers product recommendations, expresses appreciation and provides follow-up

» Care and safety guidelines for chemical exfoliation help to prevent contra-actions that could occur including:
  » Chemical burns
  » Itching and irritation
  » Dry, uncomfortable skin
  » Post inflammatory pigmentation

» The three areas of a chemical exfoliation service are:
  » Preparation – Provides a brief overview of the steps to follow *before* you begin the chemical exfoliation service.
  » Procedure – Provides an overview of the procedures that you will use *during* the chemical exfoliation service to ensure predictable results.
  » Completion – Provides an overview of the steps to follow *after* performing the chemical exfoliation service to ensure guest satisfaction

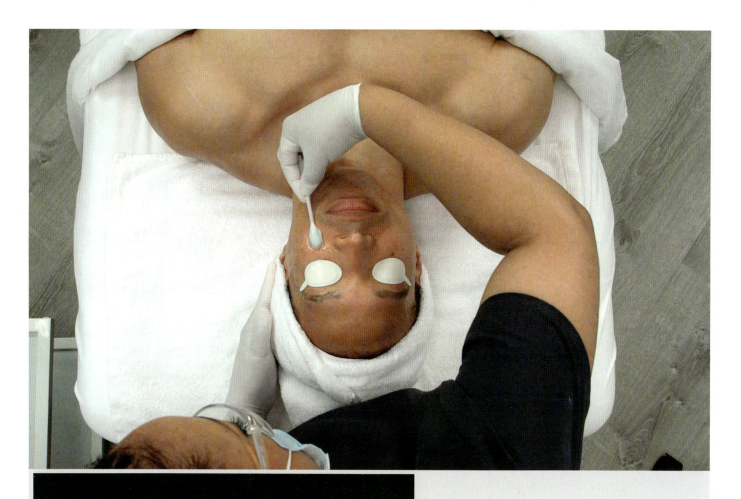

CHEMICAL EXFOLIATION

EXPLORE

What are some reactions that could happen if you incorrectly choose the strength and type of chemical peel to use on your client?

INSPIRE

One of the most powerful weapons in an esthetician's arsenal is offering chemical exfoliation treatments to improve skin texture, reduce fine lines, stimulate collagen and increase cell renewal.

ACHIEVE

Following this *Chemical Exfoliation Workshop*, you'll be able to:

» Demonstrate proper procedures to perform a chemical exfoliation treatment

CHEMICAL EXFOLIATION PROCEDURES

	TOOLS/SUPPLIES	PRODUCTS
1. PRE-CLEANSE:	headband, cotton pads, tissues, gloves	Hand Sanitizer, Makeup Remover, Cleanser
2. ANALYZE:	cotton pads, magnifying lamp, skin scope, gloves	
3. CLEANSE:	tissues, cotton pads, tissue box, gloves, cotton swabs	De-greasing product, Ointment
4. EXFOLIATE:	cotton swabs, tissue box, cotton pads, tissues	Exfoliant
5. NEUTRALIZE:	gloves, tissues	Neutralizer

FACIAL TREATMENTS

CHEMICAL EXFOLIATION PROCEDURES (CONT'D)

	TOOLS/SUPPLIES	PRODUCTS
6. MASK	fan brush, towel, cotton pads, tissues, esthetic wipes	Mask, Toner
7. PROTECT	N/A	Eye Cream, Moisturizer, Sun Protection, Serum

PERFORMANCE GUIDE
CHEMICAL EXFOLIATION
View the video, then practice the Chemical Exfoliation procedure. Complete the self-check as you progress.

60 minutes Commercially Accepted Time

PREPARATION

Wash your hands:
- Apply hand sanitizer
- Apply gloves

Note: Esthetician wears appropriate PPE at all times. Follow all applicable guidelines from regulating agencies regarding health, safety, infection control and personal protective equipment to be worn.

Set up workstation and treatment table following regulatory guidelines:
- Layered treatment-table setup

Note: Glass bowls are best for chemical exfoliants. Avoid using stainless steel bowls, which could affect the chemical.

Place fresh wet towels in hot-towel cabinet.

Perform Observe steps in the Skin Assessment and Recommendation System:
- Review client record
- Identify contraindications and cautions
- Ask about skin concerns
- Review lifestyle and health factors

Note: The client intake form and health history should be filled out before the appointment.

PRE-CLEANSE

1. Wash hands and apply gloves or apply hand sanitizer to gloves if already on.

2. Assist the client onto the treatment table and drape appropriately for treatment.

3. After the skin is pre-cleansed, place laser eye pads carefully onto each eye.

   Why do you think laser eye pads are used instead of cotton eye pads?

ANALYZE

4. Analyze the skin using magnifying lamp and Wood's lamp.

   Client analysis shows:
   - Medium to large pores throughout the forehead and nose
   - Skin on the cheeks is thick and thin around eyes
   - Wood's lamp shows small orange dots throughout the T-zone area, which indicates combination skin
   - Fitzpatrick Type 4
   - Discolored areas with some redness and fine wrinkles

   Skin conditions identified are hyperpigmentation and aging.

   The best chemical exfoliant to address these conditions is a 30% glycolic peel.

CLEANSE AND TONE

5. **Apply a degreasing product to cleanse skin:**
   » Use gauze pad working from upper chest toward forehead
   » Use long, sweeping movements until all residue is removed

   Note: Always follow manufacturer's instructions when using a degreasing product. Astringent can also be used.

6. **Blot skin thoroughly with tissue to dry.**

7. **Apply protective ointment to the sensitive areas of the face, including around the mouth, corners of the nose and around the inner eyes.**

EXFOLIATE

8. **Open the chemical exfoliant and dispense into a dish:**
   » Dispose of bottle in a covered waste bin

   Note: Do not dispense chemical exfoliant during the preparation step. This may inactivate the product.

9. The chemical exfoliant is applied evenly to the skin using 6 zones:
   » Zone 1 – Forehead
   » Zone 2 – Left cheek
   » Zone 3 – Right cheek
   » Zone 4 – Middle of face
   » Zone 5 – Jawline
   » Zone 6 – Neck and upper chest

   Note: Work quickly and be sure to fully cover each area.

10. Saturate the peel applicator, then apply product to Zone 1, the forehead, using upward movements:
    » Work across forehead from temple to temple

    Note: Before applying product, remind the client that they may feel itchiness or tingling during the chemical peeling process to manage their expectations.

11. Re-saturate applicator and apply exfoliant to Zone 2, the cheek area, to one side:
    » Use sweeping horizontal strokes from orbital bone under eye to edge of ear, moving from upper cheek to above jaw

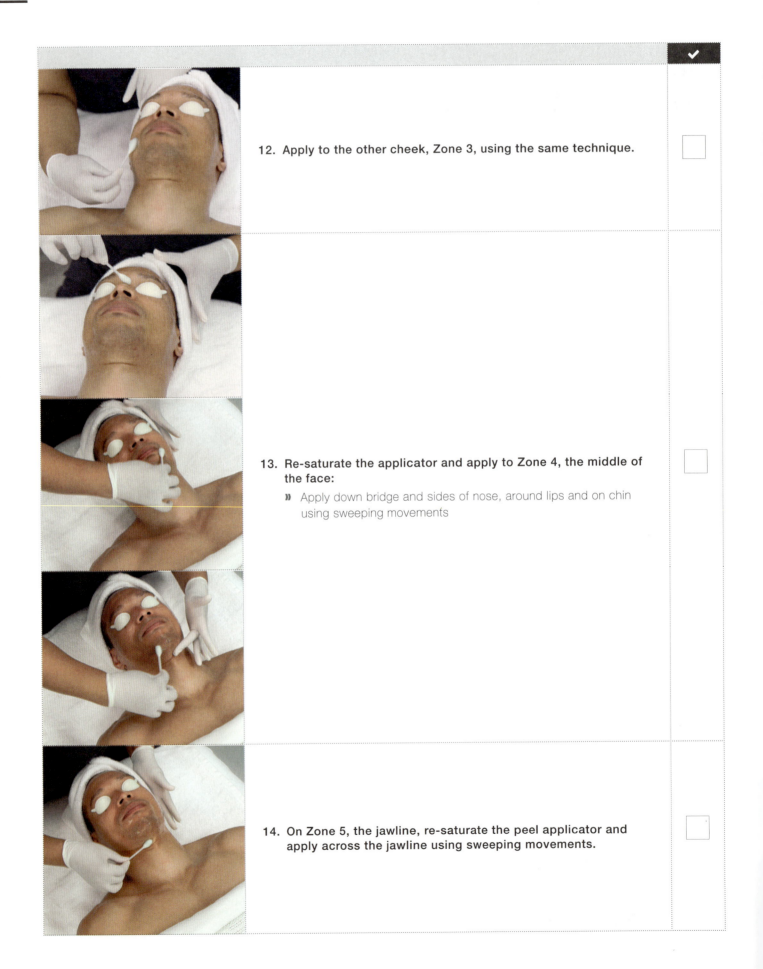

12. Apply to the other cheek, Zone 3, using the same technique.

13. Re-saturate the applicator and apply to Zone 4, the middle of the face:
    » Apply down bridge and sides of nose, around lips and on chin using sweeping movements

14. On Zone 5, the jawline, re-saturate the peel applicator and apply across the jawline using sweeping movements.

15. **Re-saturate the applicator and apply to Zone 6, the neck and upper chest:**
    » Apply sweeping motions downward, working over neck and moving across upper chest
    » Discard peel applicator

    Note: Process according to manufacturer's instructions.

NEUTRALIZE

16. **Spot-neutralize in areas of the face that process faster to prevent chemical burns.**

    Note: The skin should show mild erythema when it's ready to be neutralized. Neutralization is used for AHAs and some designer peels.

    What are some reasons why certain areas may process before the rest of the face?

17. **Saturate a gauze pad with manufacturer's recommended neutralizer or sodium bicarbonate solution:**
    » Apply to entire face until client confirms no itching or tingling is felt

    Note: Ask the client their level of sensitivity on a 0-5 scale—0 meaning they feel nothing, and 5 being more than the client can stand.

18. **After the skin has been neutralized, carefully remove the laser eye pads.**

🞊 MASK

19. Remove two towels from hot-towel cabinet and place into a bowl to cool.

20. Apply a non-setting mask to calm skin:
    » Apply from upper chest up toward forehead
    » Apply cotton eye pads to each eye

21. Remove mask using the two towels:
    » Wrap first towel over the chest and neck; wrap second towel over face
    » Gently remove mask working from forehead down to upper chest

22. Saturate gauze pad with a pH-balanced toner and apply over the entire face.

PROTECT

23. Apply eye cream first, followed by calming serum, calming moisturizer and a non-chemical SPF 30 or higher.

    Note: It is normal for a client to feel a tingling sensation when serum and moisturizer is applied.

COMPLETION

- Complete the "Teach" phase of the Skin Assessment and Recommendation system
- Include written after-care instructions that outline specific products to use within 48 hours and lifestyle cautions such as active serums such as vitamin C should be started the next day to avoid a mild burning sensation, and avoid heat and sun exposure
- Discard single-use supplies
- Disinfect tools and multi-use supplies
- Disinfect workstation and arrange in proper order
- Place used towels in a closed container or place in washing machine
- Change treatment table linens to prepare for next clien

60 minutes Commercially Accepted Time

My Speed

INSTRUCTIONS:
Record your time in comparison with the commercially accepted time. Then list here how you could improve your performance.

107ᴱ GLOSSARY/INDEX

Accutane   68
Medication used to treat severe nodular acne. Can cause extremely dry skin, itching, rash, cracks in corners of mouth. Avoid treatment.

Acid Exfoliant   21
Type of acid based on skin conditions and Fitzpatrick type. Dispense per manufacturer's instructions. Additional training is mandatory.

Acne Facial Treatment   8
A facial treatment to treat acne. The steps of the facial vary based on the products you use and the grade of acne. During the Balance phase, the massage should avoid inflamed, acneic areas.

Active Infection   68
Visuals signs include rash, swollen lymph nodes, lesions, red, swollen, pus-filled bump, abnormal sweating. Avoid treatment.

Acupressure   54
An ancient remedy of Chinese traditional medicine known to relieve pain in specific areas of the body. It consists of applying pressure to specific points of the face and body to release muscular tension, stimulate and restore balance.

Alpha-Hydroxy Acids (AHAs)   163
A term for a group of acids that occur naturally in food. These include glycolic, lactic, phytic and mandelic acids. Vary in structure, size and weight, they all have a hydroxyl group in the alpha carbon position. AHAs are considered water-soluble and must be neutralized before removing.

Analyze   5
Assessment of the skin to create a personalized treatment.

Anti-Aging Facial Treatment   13
Benefits include firming and toning, deep exfoliation, increased hydration, improved skin clarity.

Antibacterial Serum   24
Used after extraction, before mask step for breakouts.

Aromatherapy Massage   54
Allows you to combine your chosen massage technique, usually classical massage, with massage oil scented with essential oils that contain certain benefits for the body, mind, spirit.

Astringent   20
Use after second cleanse, after extraction; combination, oily, acne-prone skin.

Autoimmune Disorders   68
Visual signs include butterfly rash, bumpy, red patches covered with white scales. Avoid treatment.

Bacterial Skin Infection   68
Visual signs include red sores, honey-colored crusts, red swollen pus-filled bumps, red/pink eyes with thick mucus, red lump on eyelid with yellow spot at middle. Avoid treatment.

Balance Phase   6
The skin is prepared to receive an infusion of active ingredients to correct the skin's pH and improve the skin's hydration and protection. The modalities used to balance the skin vary depending on each client's skin analysis.

Beta-Hydroxy Acids (BHAs)   163
Also known as salicylic acid. Salicylic acid (SA) is a unique hydroxy acid since it's lipophilic. Salicylic acid penetrates the sebaceous material in the hair follicle, causing exfoliation– even in oily areas of the face and scalp.

Blended Acid   164
Popular combinations of formulations that are specific to a manufacturer. Combinations are based on the effect that the manufacturer wants to see. Some common blends are salicylic acid with low levels of TCA (trichloroacetic acid) and skin-lightening ingredients like kojic acid.

Bolster   32
Elongated cushion used to support client.

Carbolic Acid   161
A deep peel. Must be performed by a physician.

Chemical Burn   174
A contra-action that can occur during a chemical peel.

Chemical Exfoliation   *160*
Chemical peel service that improves the appearance of the skin. Most treatments improve texture, fine lines and wrinkles, pigmentation, hydration, mild scarring.

Cleaning   *26*
Removes surface or visible debris and potential pathogens to slow the growth of pathogens. Use soap, detergent or chemical "cleaner," followed by a clean-water rinse. Cleaning is performed before disinfection procedures.

Cleanse   *5, 40, 43*
The act of removing dirt, makeup and impurities from the face.

Cleansing Cream   *19*
Used for second cleanse; dry, normal skin types.

Cleansing Gel   *19*
Used for second cleanse; all skin types; prep for chemical or mechanical exfoliation.

Cleansing Milk   *19*
Used for second cleanse, all skin types.

Client Gown   *28*
Covers and allows client to remove clothing (to prevent staining).

Cocoon Wrap   *36*
Designed to create a secure and warm environment for your client.

Comedone   *6*
Small bumps frequently found on the forehead and chin associated with acne; open comedones are blackheads, closed comedones are whiteheads.

Comedone Extractor   *26*
Used to ease the removal of comedones.

Contraindications   *67*
Conditions that prevent treatment. These present in two ways Medical conditions and medications disclosed by your client or visual signs, such as some primary and secondary lesions, injury or irritation.

Decrease Phase   *6*
The goals are to reduce inflammation, microcirculation, and bacteria overgrowth. Target pigmentation concerns, erythema (redness), rough texture and edema. Decrease skin barrier dysfunction and melanocyte over-production.

Desincrustation Solution   *21*
Used before extraction to soften debris.

Desquamation   *159*
Shedding, peeling or coming off in scales.

Disinfection   *26*
Kills certain pathogens (bacteria, viruses and fungi), but not spores, on nonporous surfaces, tools and multi-use supplies. Disinfectants come in varied forms, including concentrate, liquid, spray or wipes that have EPA approval for use.

Dr. Jacquet Movement   *46*
Loosens and expels excess sebum from the follicle. The movement is used for oily and acne-blemished skin.

Effleurage   *48*
A light, rhythmic, continuous stroking or circular movement.

Enzyme   *44*
An exfoliant that is gentle enough for most skin conditions.

Erythema   *44*
Redness on the skin.

Exfoliant   *21*
Product that helps the absorption of products and improves cellular renewal.

Exfoliate   *5, 44*
Removal of dead skin cells and buildup of pollution and debris. Helps remove the top layers of the stratum corneum and aids in the absorption of the products used in the facial. Allows for deeper cleansing of the pores and encourages cellular renewal.

Exfoliating Cream   *21*
A mechanical exfoliant. Also known as gommage.

Exfoliation   *44*
Helps remove the top layers of the stratum corneum, which aids in the absorption of the products. Allows for deeper cleansing of the pores and encourages cellular renewal. Can be adapted to suit all skin types and conditions, depending on the product and how it is applied.

Express Facial Treatment 7
A condensed, 30-minute facial.

Extraction 45
The process of removing comedones from the skin.

Facial Treatment 4
A service used to improve and maintain the appearance of the face skin.

Facial Treatment Phases 5
The facial treatment is divided into three phases, with each having a specific purpose: increase, balance and decrease.

Folliculitis Barbae 10
An infection on the face and neck where the area surrounding the hair follicle is inflamed with redness and pustules. Caused by damage or blockage of the hair follicle.

Friction 45
A circular or wringing movement that moves skin over underlying structures with no gliding, usually carried out with the fingertips or palms of the hands.

Glycolic Acid 163
Can penetrate into the epidermis more effectively because it has the smallest molecular size of the AHAs.

Grades 1-2 Acne 8
Grade 1 (mild): mostly confined to whiteheads and blackheads, with a few papules and pustules; Grade 2 (moderate, or pustular acne): multiple papules and pustules, mostly confined to the face. Can receive treatment.

Grades 3-4 Acne 8
Grade 3 (moderately severe; nodulocystic acne): numerous papules and pustules; the occasional inflamed nodule; the back and the chest may also be affected. Grade 4 (severe nodulocystic acne): numerous large, painful pustules and nodules; inflammation. Cannot receive treatment without a physician's consent prior to service.

Hydrating Facial 13
A skin care treatment that provides healing and hydration to the face while stimulating and rejuvenating skin at a deeper level.

Increase Phase 5
The function of the Increase phase is to stimulate the skin, promoting cell turnover and increased skin moisture.

Insertion 47
The end of the muscle that attaches to the freely moving bone of its joint.

Jessner's Peel Solution 163
A mixture of salicylic acid, resorcinol, lactic acid and ethanol, used both for superficial and medium-depth peels, depending upon the concentration of acid and layers applied.

Laser Eye Pads 166
Shields that adhere to skin around eyes.

Layered Treatment Table Setup 37
Commonly used option for the treatment room using linens and sheets to add comfort and function to a treatment table.

Magnifying Lamp 168
Illuminates and amplifies skin to determine skin conditions.

Manual Lymph Drainage 54
A light-pressure massage for the lymphatic system to remove waste from the body. Helps with edema, erythema, puffiness, discoloration under the eyes, acne and cellulite.

Massage 47
A systematic, therapeutic method of manipulating the body by rubbing, pinching, tapping, kneading or stroking with hands, fingers or an instrument.

Men's Facial Treatment 10
A facial treatment targeted to men's concerns including the skin; pH of a male client tends to be more acidic, facial hair tends to be thick and issues with folliculitis, Oil production; testosterone promotes an active sebaceous gland.

Modality 6, 70, 71
The devices, tools and techniques used to perform a treatment.

Multi-Masking 23
Uses different masks in specific areas on the face for a customized treatment.

Neutralizer 165
Stops action of chemical exfoliant.

Origin 47
One end of a muscle, generally at the location where it attaches to a bone. The immoveable part of the muscle.

Percussion 49
A light tapping or slapping movement applied with the fingertips or partly flexed fingers. The movement is usually carried out on the body with the hands swinging freely from the wrist in a rapid motion. Also known as tapotement.

Petrissage 48
A light or heavy kneading and rolling of the muscles. It is used on the face, the arms, the shoulders and the upper back.

Phenol Peel 161
A deep peel. Must be performed by a physician.

Post-Surgery Facial 13
Procedure designed for those who have recently undergone surgery. Reduces discomfort, increases lymphatic drainage, provides deep hydration.

Pre-Cleanse 5
Light cleansing to remove any makeup before starting treatment.

Protect 6
Care given to the body to ward off impurities. An example would be adding serums to address specific concerns and moisturizing with sun protection (SPF).

Pseudofolliculitis Barbae 10
Shaving rash or razor bumps; foreign body reaction. Characterized by papules, which may be itchy. Occurs most often in men with coarse or tightly curled hair in which the hair curves back into the skin, creating inflammation of the hair follicles. Caused by ingrown hair due to incorrect shaving.

Salicylic Acid 163
A hydroxy acid that is lipophilic or attracted to oil. Penetrates the sebaceous material in the hair follicle, causing exfoliation, even in oily areas of the face and scalp. Also known as beta-hydroxy acid.

Scalp Massage 54
Head massage designed to relax the mind and encourage circulation. Helps increase circulation and amplifies the amount of red blood cells in the scalp. More red blood cells enhance growth and rejuvenation and allow the scalp to produce more hair follicles.

Skin-Brightening Facial 13
Procedure that reduces dark spots, increases hydration and provides deep exfoliation.

Soothing Facial 13
Procedure that reduces redness, irritation and provides deep hydration.

Tapotement 49
A light tapping or slapping movement applied with the fingertips or partly flexed fingers. The movement is usually carried out on the body with the hands swinging freely from the wrist in a rapid motion. Also known as percussion.

Toner 5
Lotion or wash designed to cleanse the skin and shrink the appearance of pores, usually used on the face. Refreshes the skin and balances the pH.

Treat 6
To behave toward someone or deal with something in a particular way. For example: using extractions to remove comedones.

Vibration 49
A shaking movement in the arms of the esthetician, while the fingertips or palms are touching the client.

Wood's Lamp 30, 168
Specialized filtered blacklight that allows for a more thorough skin analysis detecting problems invisible to the naked eye. Allows for identification of skin type and pigmentation conditions and any skin infection.

PIVOT POINT

ACKNOWLEDGMENTS

Pivot Point Fundamentals is designed to provide education to undergraduate students to help prepare them for licensure and an entry-level position in the esthetics field. An undertaking of this magnitude requires the expertise and cooperation of many people who are experts in their field. Pivot Point takes pride in our internal team of educators who develop esthetics, cosmetology, barbering and nails education, along with our print and digital experts, designers, editors, illustrators and video producers. Pivot Point would like to express our many thanks to these talented individuals who have devoted themselves to the business of beauty, lifelong learning and especially for help raising the bar for future professionals in our industry.

In addition, we give special thanks to the North American regulating agencies whose careful work protects us as well as our clients, enhancing the high quality of our work. These agencies include the Occupational Health and Safety Agency (OSHA) and the U.S. Environmental Protection Agency (EPA). *Pivot Point Fundamentals* promotes use of their policies and procedures.

Pivot Point International would like to express our SPECIAL THANKS to the inspired visual artisans of Creative Commons, without whose talents this book of beauty would not be possible.

EDUCATION RESEARCH
Vasiliki Stavrakis //
Janet Fisher
Jane Wegner

EDUCATION DEVELOPMENT
Sabine Held-Perez // Melissa Holmes
Markel Artwell
Brian Fallon
Lisa Luppino
Lisa Kersting
Jamie Nabielec
Vic Piccolotto
Paul Suttles

SUBJECT MATTER EXPERTS
Susanne Schmaling //
Diana Arce
Toshiana Baker
Amy Lewis
Cynthia Malcom
Leslie Roste

EDITORIAL
Maureen Spurr // Deidre Anderson // Wm. Bullion
Alyce Vacha

DESIGN & PRODUCTION
Jennifer Eckstein // Annette Baase // Agnieszka Hansen
Kimberly Miracle-Gray
Kristine Palmer
Denise Podlin
Rick Russell
Melinda Zabroski

PROJECT MANAGEMENT
Burke Broholm // Jenny Allen
Christine Goble

DIGITAL IMPLEMENTATION
John Bernin
Javed Fouch
Matt Krog
Marcia Noriega
Allenisia Roper

VIDEO & PHOTOGRAPHY
John Bernin // Jamie Nabielec
Steve Apter
Bob Long
Marc Menet

Pivot Point also wishes to take this opportunity to acknowledge the many contributors who helped make this program possible.

INDUSTRY CONTRIBUTORS

Bioelements

Jeanne Braa Foster,
Dr. Dean Foster
Eyes on Cancer

Dermaglow

Dermalogica

Dermastart

International Dermal Institute

Kaelen Harwell Organic Day Spa & Skincare Products

LightStim
LightStim.com

Pivot Point Academy

Pure Aesthetics Natural Skincare School

Clif St. Germain, Ph.D
Emeritus

Sugar Lash Inc.

Tricoci University of Beauty Culture

LEADERSHIP TEAM

Kevin Cameron
*Senior Vice President,
Sales, Marketing and Education*

Javed Fouch
*Assistant Vice President,
Technology Operations
and Learning Technology*

Sabine Held-Perez
*Assistant Vice President,
Education Strategy
and Development*

Jan Laan
*Vice President, International
Business Development*

Katy O'Mahony
*Assistant Vice President,
Human Resources*

Robert Passage
Chairman and CEO

Robert J. Sieh
*Senior Vice President,
Finance and Operations*

This work is based in part on previously copyrighted materials owned by Pivot Point International, Inc., including:

Salon Fundamentals Esthetics
© 2004 Pivot Point International, Inc.
All rights reserved.
ISBN-13: 978-0-9742723-1-3
ISBN-10: 0-9742723-1-0
1st Edition
1st Printing, February 2004
Printed in Hong Kong

Pivot Point Fundamentals: Cosmetology
© 2016 Pivot Point International, Inc.
All rights reserved.
ISBN 978-1-940593-56-2
1st Edition
1st Printing, November 2016
Printed in Hong Kong

*Pivot Point Fundamentals:
Beauty Therapy – Level 2*
© 2019 Pivot Point International, Inc.
All rights reserved.
1st Edition
1st Printing, June 2019

#MOOD

inspiration:

NOTES:

goals:

spas i like:

@pivotpointintl
#pivotpoint
#learnforward
#pivotpointesthetics

#MOOD